Introduction to Ethics

3600:120-009

Instructor

Mr. Ian D. MacKinnon

create.mheducation.com

ISBN-13: 9780390718280

ISBN-10: 0390718289

Contents

Anthropology and the Abnormal

Ruth Benedict

Ruth Benedict was born Ruth Fulton in 1887 in New York City. She attended Vassar College in Poughkeepsie, New York, receiving a degree in English literature in 1909. She then taught English in high school and wrote poetry under the pseudonym Anne Singleton. In 1914 she married Stanley Benedict, a biochemist. She later became interested in anthropology, and in 1923 earned her doctoral degree in this field from Columbia University, writing her dissertation on the concept of the guardian spirit among native North Americans. She had begun teaching at Columbia in 1922 and was promoted to assistant professor in 1930. In 1934 she published *Patterns of Culture*, a study of the diversity of cultures that focused on the Zuñi (in New Mexico), the Kwakiutl (on the northwest coast of North America), and the Dobuans (on the island of Dobu, near New Guinea). Later publications include *Zuñi Mythology* (1935), *Race: Science and Politics* (1940; 2d ed., 1943), and *The Chrysanthemum and the Sword: Patterns of Japanese Culture* (1946). She became a professor at Columbia in 1948, and died in New York City later that year.

    Our reading is from Benedict's 1934 article, "Anthropology and the Abnormal." Benedict argues that the psychological categories of "normal" and "abnormal" are not absolute but are defined by culture. Anthropological research indicates that every kind of behavior that we, from the perspective of our Western European culture, consider abnormal, is considered normal (and even honored) in some other society. For example, the Dobuans think that extreme suspicion of everyone (what we would call paranoia) is normal, and view friendliness (which we value) as an aberration. "Normality" means the general way a given culture happens to live out one of the many possible patterns of human behavior; "abnormality" refers to patterns not adopted by a culture. Normality and abnormality, that is to say, are relative rather than absolute.

    The concept of the moral, Benedict explains, is a variant of the concept of the normal. Like normality, moral values are not absolute but relative to culture: Morality is "a convenient term for socially approved habits." Nonetheless, further research might show that "a modicum of what is considered right and wrong" is shared by all cultures.

▼

Modern social anthropology has become more and more a study of the varieties and common elements of cultural environment and the consequences of these in human behavior. For such a study of diverse social orders, primitive peoples fortunately provide a laboratory not yet entirely vitiated by the spread of a standardized worldwide civilization. Dyaks and Hopis, Fijians and Yakuts, are significant for psychological and sociological study because only among these simpler peoples has there been sufficient isolation to give opportunity for the development of localized social

"Anthropology and the Abnormal" by Ruth Benedict from *Journal of General Psychology*, Volume 10, Number 1, 1934. Reprinted with the permission of the Helen Dwight Reid Educational Foundation. Published by Heldref Publications, 1319 Eighteenth Street, N.W., Washington, D.C. 20036-1802. Copyright © 1934.

forms. In the higher cultures the standardization of custom and belief over a couple of continents has given a false sense of the inevitability of the particular forms that have gained currency, and we need to turn to a wider survey in order to check the conclusions we hastily base upon this near-universality of familiar customs. Most of the simpler cultures did not gain the wide currency of the one which, out of our experience, we identify with human nature, but this was for various historical reasons, and certainly not for any that gives us as its carriers a monopoly of social good or of social sanity. Modern civilization, from this point or view, becomes not a necessary pinnacle of human achievement but one entry in a long series of possible adjustments.

These adjustments, whether they are in mannerisms like the ways of showing anger or joy or grief in any society, or in major human drives like those of sex, prove to be far more variable than experience in any one culture would suggest. In certain fields, such as that of religion or of formal marriage arrangements, these wide limits of variability are well known and can be fairly described. In others it is not yet possible to give a generalized account, but that does not absolve us of the task of indicating the significance of the work that has been done and of the problems that have arisen.

One of these problems relates to the customary modern normal-abnormal categories and our conclusions regarding them. In how far are such categories culturally determined, or in how far can we with assurance regard them as absolute? In how far can we regard inability to function socially as diagnostic of abnormality, or in how far is it necessary to regard this as a function of the culture?

As a matter of fact, one of the most striking facts that emerge from a study of widely varying cultures is the ease with which our abnormals function in other cultures. It does not matter what kind of "abnormality" we choose for illustration, those which indicate extreme instability, or those which are more in the nature of character traits like sadism or delusions of grandeur or of persecution; there are well-described cultures in which these abnormals function at ease and with honor, and apparently without danger or difficulty to the society.

The most notorious of these are trance and catalepsy. Even a very mild mystic is aberrant in our culture. But most peoples have regarded even extreme psychic manifestations not only as normal and desirable, but even as characteristic of highly valued and gifted individuals. This was true even in our own cultural background in that period when Catholicism made the ecstatic experience the mark of sainthood. It is hard for us, born and brought up in a culture that makes no use of the experience, to realize how important a role it may play and how many individuals are capable of it, once it has been given an honorable place in any society....

Cataleptic and trance phenomena are, of course, only one illustration of the fact that those whom we regard as abnormals may function adequately in other cultures. Many of our culturally discarded traits are selected for elaboration in different societies. Homosexuality is an excellent example, for in this case our attention is not constantly diverted, as in the consideration of trance, to the interruption of routine activity which it implies. Homosexuality poses the problem very simply. A tendency toward this trait in our culture exposes an individual to all the conflicts to which all aberrants are always exposed, and we tend to identify the consequences of this conflict with homosexuality. But these consequences are obviously local and cultural. Homosexuals in many societies are not incompetent, but they may be such if the culture asks adjustments of them that would strain any man's vitality. Wherever homosexuality has been given an honorable place in any society, those to whom it is congenial have filled adequately the honorable roles society assigns to them. Plato's *Republic* is, of course, the most convincing statement of such a reading of homosexuality. It is presented as one of the major means to the good life, and it was generally so regarded in Greece at that time.

The cultural attitude toward homosexuals has not always been on such a high ethical plane, but it has been very varied. Among many American Indian tribes there exists the institution of the berdache, as the French called them. These men-women were men who at puberty or thereafter took the dress and the occupations of women. Sometimes they married other men and lived with them. Sometimes they were men with no inversion,[1] persons of weak sexual endowment who chose this role to avoid the jeers of the women. The berdaches were never regarded as of first-rate supernatural power, as similar men-women were in Siberia, but rather as leaders in women's occupations, good healers in certain diseases, or, among certain tribes, as the genial organizers of social affairs. In any case, they were socially placed. They were not left exposed to the conflicts that visit the deviant who is excluded from participation in the recognized patterns of his society.

The most spectacular illustrations of the extent to which normality may be culturally defined are those cultures where an abnormality of our culture is the cornerstone of their social structure. It is not possible to do justice to these possibilities in a short discussion. A recent study of an island of northwest Melanesia by Fortune[2] describes a society built upon traits which we regard as beyond the border of paranoia. In this tribe the exogamic[3] groups look upon each other as prime manipulators of black magic, so that one marries always into an enemy group which remains for life one's deadly and unappeasable foes. They look upon a good garden crop as a confession of theft, for everyone is engaged in making magic to induce into his garden the productiveness of his neighbors; therefore no secrecy in the island is so rigidly insisted upon as the secrecy of a man's harvesting of his yams. Their polite phrase at the acceptance of a gift is, "And if you now poison me, how shall I repay you this present?" Their preoccupation with poisoning is constant; no woman ever leaves her cooking pot for a moment untended. Even the great affinal[4] economic exchanges that are characteristic of this Melanesian culture area are quite altered in Dobu since they are incompatible with this fear and distrust that pervades the culture. They go farther and people the whole world outside their own quarters with such malignant spirits that all-night feasts and ceremonials simply do not occur here. They have even rigorous religiously enforced customs that forbid the sharing of seed even in one family group. Anyone else's food is deadly poison to you, so that communality of stores is out of the question. For some months before harvest the whole society is on the verge of starvation, but if one falls to the temptation and eats up one's seed yams, one is an outcast and a beachcomber for life. There is no coming back. It involves, as a matter of course, divorce and the breaking of all social ties.

Now in this society where no one may work with another and no one may share with another, Fortune describes the individual who was regarded by all his fellows as crazy. He was not one of those who periodically ran amok and, beside himself and frothing at the mouth, fell with a knife upon anyone he could reach. Such behavior they did not regard as putting anyone outside the pale. They did not even put the individuals who were known to be liable to these attacks under any kind of control. They merely fled when they saw the attack coming on and kept out of the way. "He would be all right tomorrow." But there was one man of sunny, kindly disposition who liked work and liked to be helpful. The compulsion was too strong for him to repress it in favor of the opposite tendencies of his culture. Men and women never spoke of him without laughing; he was silly and simple and definitely crazy. Nevertheless, to the ethnologist used to a culture that has, in Christianity, made his type the model of all virtue, he seemed a pleasant fellow. . . .

Among the Kwakiutl it did not matter whether a relative had died in bed of disease, or by the hand of an enemy; in either case death was an affront to be wiped out by the death of another person. The fact that one had been caused to mourn was proof that one had been put upon. A chief's sister and her daughter had gone up to Victoria, and either because they drank bad whiskey or because their boat capsized, they never came back.

The chief called together his warriors. "Now I ask you, tribes, who shall wail? Shall I do it or shall another?" The spokesman answered, of course, "Not you, Chief. Let some other of the tribes." Immediately they set up the war pole to announce their intention of wiping out the injury and gathered a war party. They set out and found seven men and two children asleep and killed them. "Then they felt good when they arrived at Sebaa in the evening."

The point which is of interest to us is that in our society those who on that occasion would feel good when they arrived at Sebaa that evening would be the definitely abnormal. There would be some, even in our society, but it is not a recognized and approved mood under the circumstances. . . .

This head-hunting that takes place on the Northwest Coast after a death is no matter of blood revenge or of organized vengeance. There is no effort to tie up the subsequent killing with any responsibility on the part of the victim for the death of the person who is being mourned. A chief whose son has died goes visiting wherever his fancy dictates, and he says to his host, "My prince has died today, and you go with him." Then he kills him. In this, according to their interpretation, he acts nobly because he has not been downed. He has thrust back in return. The whole procedure is meaningless without the fundamental paranoid reading of bereavement. Death, like all the other untoward accidents of existence, confounds man's pride and can only be handled in the category of insults. . . .

These illustrations, which it has been possible to indicate only in the briefest manner, force upon us the fact that normality is culturally defined. An adult shaped to the drives and standards of either of these cultures, if he were transported into our civilization, would fall into our categories of abnormality. He would be faced with the psychic dilemmas of the socially unavailable. In his own culture, however, he is the pillar of society, the end result of socially inculcated mores,[5] and the problem of personal instability in his case simply does not arise.

No one civilization can possibly utilize in its mores the whole potential range of human behavior. Just as there are great numbers of possible phonetic articulations, and the possibility of language depends on a selection and standardization of a few of these in order that speech communication may be possible at all, so the possibility of organized behavior of every sort, from the fashions of local dress and houses to the dicta[6] of a people's ethics and religion, depends upon a similar selection among the possible behavior traits. In the field of recognized economic obligations or sex tabus, this selection is as nonrational and subconscious a process as it is in the field of phonetics. It is a process which goes on in the group for long periods of time and is historically conditioned by innumerable accidents of isolation or of contact of peoples. In any comprehensive study of psychology, the selection that different cultures have made in the course of history within the great circumference of potential behavior is of great significance.

Every society, beginning with some slight inclination in one direction or another, carries its preference farther and farther, integrating itself more and more completely upon its chosen basis and discarding those types of behavior that are uncongenial. Most of those organizations of personality that seem to us most incontrovertibly abnormal have been used by different civilizations in the very foundations of their institutional life. Conversely, the most valued traits of our normal individuals have been looked on in differently organized cultures as aberrant. Normality, in short, within a very wide range, is culturally defined. It is primarily a term for the socially elaborated segment of human behavior in any culture; and abnormality, a term for the segment that that particular civilization does not use. The very eyes with which we see the problem are conditioned by the long traditional habits of our own society.

It is a point that has been made more often in relation to ethics than in relation to psychiatry. We do not any longer make the mistake of deriving the morality of our own locality and decade directly from the inevitable constitution of human nature. We do not elevate it to the dignity of a first principle. We recognize that morality differs in every society, and is a convenient term for socially approved habits. Mankind has always preferred to say "It is morally good" rather than "It is habitual," and the fact of this preference is matter enough for a critical science of ethics. But historically the two phrases are synonymous.

The concept of the normal is properly a variant of the concept of the good. It is that which society has approved. A normal action is one which falls well within the limits of expected behavior for a particular society. Its variability among different peoples is essentially a function of the variability of the behavior patterns that different societies have created for themselves, and can never be wholly divorced from a consideration of culturally institutionalized types of behavior.

Each culture is a more or less elaborate working-out of the potentialities of the segment [of possible human behaviors] it has chosen. Insofar as a civilization is well integrated and consistent within itself, it will tend to carry farther and farther, according to its nature, its initial impulse toward a particular type of action, and from the point of view of any other culture those elaborations will include more and more extreme and aberrant traits.

Each of these traits, in proportion as it reinforces the chosen behavior patterns of that culture, is for that culture normal. Those individuals to whom it is congenial, either congenitally or as the result of childhood sets, are accorded prestige in that culture and are not visited with the social contempt or disapproval which their traits would call down upon them in a society that was differently organized. On the other hand, those individuals whose characteristics are not congenial to the selected type of human behavior in that community are the deviants, no matter how valued their personality traits may be in a contrasted civilization. . . .

I have spoken of individuals as having sets toward certain types of behavior, and of these sets as running sometimes counter to the types of behavior which are institutionalized in the culture to which they belong. From all that we know of contrasting cultures, it seems clear that differences of temperament occur in every society. The matter has never been made the subject of investigation, but from the available material it would appear that these temperament types are very likely of universal recurrence. That is, there is an ascertainable range of human behavior that is found wherever a sufficiently large series of individuals is observed. But the proportion in which behavior types stand to one another in different societies is not universal. The vast majority of the individuals in any group are shaped to the fashion of that culture. In other words, most individuals are plastic to the molding force of the society into which they are born. In a society that values trance, as in India, they will have supernormal experience. In a society that institutionalizes homosexuality, they will be homosexual. In a society that sets the gathering of possessions as the chief human objective, they will amass property. The deviants, whatever the type of behavior the culture has institutionalized, will remain few in number, and there seems no more difficulty in molding the vast malleable majority to the "normality" of what we consider an aberrant trait, such as delusions of reference, than to the normality of such accepted behavior patterns as acquisitiveness. The small proportion of the number of the deviants in any culture is not a function of the sure instinct with which that society has built itself upon the fundamental sanities, but of the universal fact that, happily, the majority of mankind quite readily take any shape that is presented to them. . . .

The problem of understanding abnormal human behavior in any absolute sense independent of cultural factors is still far in the future. The categories of borderline behavior which we derive from the study of the neuroses and psychoses of our civilization are categories of prevailing local types of instability. They give much information about the stresses and strains of Western civilization, but no final picture of inevitable human behavior. Any conclusions about such behavior must await the collection by trained observers of psychiatric data from other cultures. Since no adequate work of the kind has been done at the present time, it is impossible to say what core or definition of abnormality may be found valid from the comparative material. It is as it is in ethics: all our local conventions of moral behavior and of immoral are without absolute validity, and yet it is quite possible that a modicum of what is considered right and what wrong could be disentangled that is shared by the whole human race.

▶ NOTES

1. *inversion:* male homosexuality. [D.C.A., ed.]
2. R. F. Fortune, *Sorcerers of Dobu: The Social Anthropology of the Dobu Islanders* (New York: E. P. Dutton, 1932). [R.B.]
3. *exogamic:* marrying persons outside the group. [D.C.A.]
4. *affinal:* based on marriage. [D.C.A.]
5. *mores:* morally binding customs. [D.C.A.]
6. *dicta:* authoritative pronouncements. [D.C.A.]

Letter to Menoeceus

Epicurus

Epicurus was born of Athenian parents in 341 B.C.E. on Samos, an island off the coast of Asia Minor. At fourteen he began studying philosophy under Pamphilius, a follower of Plato. He then spent three years at Teos, a city on the coast of Asia Minor, as a student of Nausiphanes, who was a disciple of Democritus. When he was eighteen, Epicurus went to Athens to serve two years in the military (a requirement for Athenian citizenship). He then rejoined his parents, who had moved to Colophon in western Asia Minor. Epicurus continued to study philosophy and in 311 established a school at Mytilene, a city on the island of Lesbos. He later set up a school at Lampsacus, on the Hellespont. In 307, accompanied by his followers, Epicurus came to Athens and purchased a house. The house had a garden, and this became the site of Epicurus's school. The school was a community of men and women—and at least one slave—who lived according to the master's teachings. Epicurus headed the community (which came to be called "the Garden") until he died in 270, at the age of seventy-two.

Most of Epicurus's writings have been lost. What remains is a collection of his sayings known as the *Principal Doctrines,* another collection called *The Vatican Sayings* (so named because the manuscript is in the Vatican Library), fragments of his treatise *On Nature,* a letter to Herodotus, and a letter to Menoeceus. An additional work, in the form of a letter from Epicurus to Pythocles, seems to be have been written by a disciple.

Our reading is the *Letter to Menoeceus.* Epicurus sets forth for Menoeceus his central teachings pertaining to the proper conduct of life. (1) The gods exist, are immortal and blessed, and take pleasure in human beings who are like themselves. (2) It is foolish to fear death, since death is nothing when we are alive (it has not yet come) and nothing when we are dead (since we no longer exist). (3) The first principle and goal of a happy life is pleasure, which is not sensual indulgence (as Epicurus's detractors misrepresent his doctrine) but "the absence of pain in the body and of trouble in the soul." (4) The fundamental virtue is prudence, which enables us to choose pleasures intelligently. (5) We are responsible for our actions and are not ruled by necessity or chance.

Epicurus to Menoeceus:[1] Greeting.

Let no one be slow to seek wisdom when he is young nor weary in the search [of it] when he is grown old. For no age is too early or too late for the health of the soul. And to say that the season for studying philosophy has not yet come, or that it is past and gone, is like saying that the season for happiness is not yet or that it is now no more. Therefore both old and young ought to seek wisdom, the former in order that, as age comes over him, he may be young in good things because of the grace of what has been; and the latter in order that, while he is young, he may at the same time be old, because he has no fear of the things which are to come. So we must exercise ourselves in the things which bring happiness, since, if that be present, we have everything, and, if that be absent, all our actions are directed toward attaining it.

Those things which without ceasing I have declared to you, those do, and exercise yourself [in them], holding them to be the elements of right life. First, believe that God is a living being immortal and blessed, according to the notion of a god indicated by the common sense of mankind. And so believing, you shall not affirm of him aught that is foreign to his immortality or that agrees not with blessedness, but shall believe about him whatever may uphold both his blessedness and his immortality. For verily there are gods, and the knowledge of them is manifest; but they are not such as the multitude believe, seeing that men do not steadfastly maintain the notions they form respecting them. Not the man who denies the gods worshipped by the multitude, but he who affirms of the gods what the multitude believes about them, is truly impious. For the utterances of the multitude about the gods are not true preconceptions but false assumptions. Hence it is that the greatest evils happen to the wicked and the greatest blessings happen to the good from the hand of the gods, seeing that they are always favourable to their own good qualities and take pleasure in men like unto themselves, but reject as alien whatever is not of their kind.

Accustom yourself to believe that death is nothing to us, for good and evil imply sentience, and death is the privation of all sentience. Therefore a right understanding that death is nothing to us makes the mortality of life enjoyable, not by adding to life an illimitable time, but by taking away the yearning after immortality. For life has no terrors for him who has thoroughly apprehended that there are no terrors for him in ceasing to live. Foolish, therefore, is the man who says that he fears death, not because it will pain when it comes, but because it pains in the prospect. Whatever causes no annoyance when it is present, causes only a groundless pain in the expectation. Death, therefore, the most awful of evils, is nothing to us, seeing that when we are, death is not come; and when death is come, we are not. It is nothing, then, either to the living or to the dead, for with the living it is not, and the dead exist no longer. But in the world, at one time men shun death as the greatest of all evils, and at another time choose it as a respite from the evils in life. The wise man does not deprecate life nor does he fear the cessation of life. The thought of life is no offence to him, nor is the cessation of life regarded as an evil. And even as men choose of food not merely and simply the larger portion, but the more pleasant, so the wise seek to enjoy the time which is most pleasant and not merely that which is longest. And he who admonishes the young to live well and the old to make a good end speaks foolishly, not merely because of the desirableness of life, but because the same exercise at once teaches to live well and to die well. Much worse is he who says that it were good not to be born, but when once one is born to pass with all speed through the gates of Hades. For if he truly believes this, why does he not depart from life? It were easy for him to do so, if once he were firmly convinced. If he speaks only in mockery, his words are foolishness—for those who hear, believe him not.

We must remember that the future is neither wholly ours nor wholly not ours, so that neither must we count upon it as quite certain to come, nor despair of it as quite certain not to come.

We must also reflect that, of desires, some are natural, others are groundless; and that of the natural some are necessary as well as natural, and some natural only. And of the necessary desires, some are necessary if we are to be happy, some if the body is to be rid of uneasiness, some if we are even to live. He who has a clear and certain understanding of these things will direct every preference and aversion toward securing health of body and tranquillity of mind, seeing that this is the sum and end of a blessed life. For the end of all our actions is to be free from pain and fear, and, when once we have attained all this, the tempest of the soul is laid—seeing that the living creature has no need to go in search of something that is lacking, nor to look for anything else by which the good of the soul and of the body will be fulfilled. When we are pained because of the absence of pleasure, then—and then only—do we feel the need of pleasure. Therefore we call pleasure the [first principle and the goal] of a blessed life. Pleasure is our first and kindred good. It is the starting-point of every choice and of every aversion, and to it we come back, inasmuch as we make feeling the rule by which to judge of every good thing. And since pleasure is our first and native good, for that reason we do not choose every pleasure whatsoever, but often pass over many pleasures when a greater annoyance ensues from them. And often we consider pains superior to pleasures when submission to the pains for a long time brings us as a consequence a greater pleasure. While therefore all pleasure, because it is naturally akin to us, is good; not all pleasure is choiceworthy—just as all pain is an evil, and yet not all pain is to be shunned. It is, however, by measuring one against another, and by looking at the conveniences and inconveniences, that all these matters must be judged. Sometimes we treat the good as an evil, and the evil, on the contrary, as a good. Again, we regard [being independent] of outward things as a great good, not so as in all cases to use little, but so as to be contented with little if we have not much, being honestly persuaded that they have the sweetest enjoyment of luxury who stand least in need of it, and that whatever is natural is easily procured and only the vain and worthless hard to win. Plain fare gives as much pleasure as a costly diet, when once the pain of want has been removed, while bread and water confer the highest possible pleasure when they are brought to hungry lips. To habituate oneself, therefore, to simple and inexpensive diet supplies all that is needful for health and enables a man to meet the necessary requirements of life without shrinking, and it places us in a better condition when we approach at intervals a costly fare and renders us fearless of fortune.

When we say, then, that pleasure is the end and aim, we do not mean the pleasures of the prodigal or the pleasures of sensuality, as we are understood to do by some through ignorance, prejudice, or wilful misrepresentation. By pleasure we mean the absence of pain in the body and of trouble in the soul. It is not an unbroken succession of drinking-bouts and of revelry, not sexual love, not the enjoyment of the fish and other delicacies of a luxurious table, which produce a pleasant life; it is sober reasoning, searching out the grounds of every choice and avoidance, and banishing those beliefs through which the greatest tumults take possession of the soul. Of all this the beginning and the greatest good is prudence. Therefore prudence is a more precious thing even than philosophy; from it spring all the other virtues, for it teaches that we cannot lead a life of pleasure which is not also a life of prudence, honour, and justice; nor lead a life of prudence, honour, and justice, which is not also a life of pleasure. For the virtues have grown into one with a pleasant life, and a pleasant life is inseparable from them.

Who, then, is superior in your judgement to such a man? He holds a holy belief concerning the gods and is altogether free from the fear of death. He has diligently considered the end fixed by nature and understands how easily the limit of good things can be reached and attained, and how either the duration or the intensity of evils is but slight. Destiny, which some introduce as sovereign over all things, he laughs to scorn, affirming rather that some things happen of necessity, others by chance, others through our own agency. For he sees that necessity destroys responsibility and that chance or fortune is inconstant; whereas our own actions are free, and it is to them that praise and blame naturally attach. It were better, indeed, to accept the legends of the gods than to bow beneath that yoke of destiny which the natural philosophers[2] have imposed. The one holds out some faint hope that we may escape if we honour the gods, while the necessity of the naturalists is deaf to all entreaties. Nor does he hold chance to be a god, as the world in general does, for in the acts of a god there is no disorder; nor to be a cause, though an uncertain one, for he believes that no good or evil is dispensed by chance to men so as to make life blessed, though it supplies the starting-point of great good and great evil. He believes that the misfortune of the wise is better than the prosperity of the fool. It is better, in short, that what is well judged in action should not owe its successful issue to the aid of chance.

Exercise yourself in these and kindred precepts day and night, both by yourself and with him who is like you; then never, either in waking or in dream, will you be disturbed, but will live as a god among men. For man loses all semblance of mortality by living in the midst of immortal blessings.

▶ NOTES

1. Nothing is known about Menoeceus. [D.C.A., ed.]

2. *natural philosophers:* philosophers of nature; natural scientists [D.C.A.]

Utilitarianism

John Stuart Mill

John Stuart Mill was born in London in 1806. He was educated personally by his father, the Scottish economist and philosopher James Mill, who put him through a rigorous program of study from his earliest years. Mill was reading Greek at age three and Latin at age eight. As a boy he read works of many classical authors in the original language, including works by Plato and Aristotle. When he was thirteen, he began studying the economic theories of Adam Smith and David Ricardo. The following year he traveled to France and spent a year with the family of Samuel Bentham (brother of the English jurist and philosopher Jeremy Bentham). After returning to England, he began to study Roman law, with a view to possibly becoming a lawyer. But in 1823, when he was seventeen, he took a job at the British East India Company, where he was employed for the next thirty-five years. Mill was elected to Parliament in 1865, but failed to gain reelection in 1868. After his defeat he retired to Avignon, France, where he died in 1873.

Mill's major writings include *A System of Logic* (1843), *Principles of Political Economy* (1848), *On Liberty* (1859), *Utilitarianism* (published serially in *Fraser's Magazine* in 1861, separately in 1863), and *The Subjection of Women* (written in 1861, published in 1869).

Our reading is from *Utilitarianism,* the work that has become the most popular and influential treatment of utilitarianism. Utilitarianism is the moral theory that was first set forth by Jeremy Bentham. It claims that the morality of an action is determined by how well it promotes "utility," which is defined as the greatest good for the greatest number. Utilitarians differ, however, on how to define "good" and whom to include in the "greatest number."

According to Mill, "good" means happiness, and happiness means pleasure and the absence of pain; the "greatest number" includes not only human beings but all creatures capable of feeling pleasure and pain. Mill's version of utilitarianism, therefore, claims that the moral thing to do in any situation is the action that causes the greatest sum total of pleasure for all the sentient beings involved. Mill typically says that utility is to be determined wholly on the basis of the *individual action,* but at times he seems to endorse the view that one should always follow the *rule* (for example, "Don't kill innocent people") that, when universally followed, would promote the greatest utility—even if, in a particular situation, following the rule would not do so. Philosophers have come to call these two versions of utilitarianism, respectively, *act utilitarianism* and *rule utilitarianism.*

In our selection from Chapter II, "What Utilitarianism Is," Mill briefly describes his theory and then defends it against several objections. In the selection from Chapter IV, "Of What Sort of Proof the Principle of Utility Is Susceptible," he explains in what sense one can prove that the happiness (pleasure) of the individual and the group are desirable and are the only things desirable.

▼

Chapter II: What Utilitarianism Is

. . . The creed which accepts as the foundation of morals, utility, or the greatest happiness principle, holds that actions are right in proportion as they tend to promote happiness, wrong as they tend to produce the reverse of happiness. By happiness is intended pleasure and the absence of pain; by unhappiness, pain and the privation of pleasure. To give a clear view of the moral standard set up by the theory, much more requires to be said; in particular, what things it includes in the ideas of pain and pleasure; and to what extent this is left an open question. But these supplementary explanations do not affect the theory of life on which this theory of morality is grounded—namely, that pleasure and freedom from pain are the only things desirable as ends; and that all desirable things (which are as numerous in the utilitarian as in any other scheme) are desirable either for the pleasure inherent in themselves, or as means to the promotion of pleasure and the prevention of pain.

Now such a theory of life excites in many minds, and among them in some of the most estimable in feeling and purpose, inveterate dislike. To suppose that life has (as they express it) no higher end than pleasure—no better and nobler object of desire and pursuit—they designate as utterly mean and grovelling; as a doctrine worthy only of swine, to whom the followers of Epicurus[1] were, at a very early period, contemptuously likened; and modern holders of the doctrine are occasionally made the subject of equally polite comparisons by its German, French, and English assailants.

When thus attacked, the Epicureans have always answered that it is not they, but their accusers, who represent human nature in a degrading light; since the accusation supposes human beings to be capable of no pleasures except those of which swine are capable. If this supposition were true, the charge could not be gainsaid, but would then be no longer an imputation; for if the sources of pleasure were precisely the same to human beings and to swine, the rule of life which is good enough for the one would be good enough for the other. The comparison of the Epicurean life to that of beasts is felt as degrading, precisely because a beast's pleasures do not satisfy a human being's conceptions of happiness. Human beings have faculties more elevated than the animal appetites, and when once made conscious of them, do not regard anything as happiness which does not include their gratification. I do not, indeed, consider the Epicureans to have been by any means faultless in drawing out their scheme of consequences from the utilitarian principle. To do this in any sufficient manner, many Stoic,[2] as well as Christian elements require to be included. But there is no known Epicurean theory of life which does not assign to the pleasures of the intellect, of the feelings and imagination, and of the moral sentiments, a much higher value as pleasures than to those of mere sensation. It must be admitted, however, that utilitarian writers in general have placed the superiority of mental over bodily pleasures chiefly in the greater permanency, safety, uncostliness, etc., of the former—that is, in their circumstantial advantages rather than in their intrinsic nature.[3] And on all these points utilitarians have fully proved their case; but they might have taken the other, and, as it may be called, higher ground, with entire consistency. It is quite compatible with the principle of utility to recognise the fact, that some *kinds* of pleasure are more desirable and more valuable than others. It would be absurd that while, in estimating all other things, quality is considered as well as quantity, the estimation of pleasures should be supposed to depend on quantity alone.

If I am asked what I mean by difference of quality in pleasures, or what makes one pleasure more valuable than another, merely as a pleasure, except its being greater in amount, there is but one possible answer. Of two pleasures, if there be one to which all or almost all who have experience of both give a decided preference, irrespective of any feeling of moral obligation to prefer it, that is the more desirable pleasure. If one of the two is, by those who are competently acquainted with both, placed so far above the other that they prefer it, even though knowing it to be attended with a greater amount of discontent, and would not resign it for any quantity of the other pleasure which their nature is capable of, we are justified in ascribing to the preferred enjoyment a superiority in quality, so far outweighing quantity as to render it, in comparison, of small account.

Now it is an unquestionable fact that those who are equally acquainted with, and equally capable of appreciating and enjoying, both, do give a most marked preference to the manner of existence which employs their higher faculties. Few human creatures would consent to be changed into any of the lower animals, for a promise of the fullest allowance of a beast's pleasures; no intelligent human being would consent to be a fool, no instructed person would be an ignoramus, no person of feeling and conscience would be selfish and base, even though they should be persuaded that the fool, the dunce, or the rascal is better satisfied with his lot than they are with theirs. They would not resign what they possess more than he for the most complete satisfaction of all the desires which they have in common with him. If they ever fancy they would, it is only in cases of unhappiness so extreme that to escape from it they would exchange their lot for almost any other, however undesirable in their own eyes. A being of higher faculties requires more to make him happy, is capable probably of more acute suffering, and is certainly accessible to it at more points, than one of an inferior type; but in spite of these liabilities, he can never really wish to sink into what he feels to be a lower grade of existence. We may give what explanation we please of this unwillingness; we may attribute it to pride, a name which is given indiscriminately to some of the most and to some of the least estimable feelings of which mankind are capable; we may refer it to the love of liberty and personal independence, an appeal to which was with the Stoics one of the most effective means for the inculcation of it; to the love of power, or to the love of excitement, both of which do really enter into and contribute to it. But its most appropriate appellation is a sense of dignity, which all human beings possess in one form or other and in some, though by no means in exact, proportion to their higher faculties; and which is so essential a part of the happiness of those in whom it is strong, that nothing which conflicts with it could be, otherwise than momentarily, an object of desire to them. Whoever supposes that this preference takes place at a sacrifice of happiness—that the superior being, in anything like equal circumstances, is not happier than the inferior—confounds the two very different ideas of happiness and content. It is indisputable that the being whose capacities of enjoyment are low has the greatest chance of having them fully satisfied; and a highly-endowed being will always feel that any happiness which he can look for, as the world is constituted, is imperfect. But he can learn to bear its imperfections, if they are at all bearable; and they will not make him envy the being who is indeed unconscious of the imperfections, but only because he feels not at all the good which those imperfections qualify. It is better to be a human being dissatisfied than a pig satisfied; better to be Socrates dissatisfied than a fool satisfied. And if the fool or the pig is of a different opinion, it is because they only know their own side of the question. The other party to the comparison knows both sides. . . .

I have dwelt on this point, as being a necessary part of a perfectly just conception of utility or happiness, considered as the directive rule of human conduct. But it is by no means an indispensable condition to the acceptance of the utilitarian standard; for that standard is not the agent's own greatest happiness, but the greatest amount of happiness altogether; and if it may possibly be doubted whether a noble character is always the happier for its nobleness, there can be no doubt that it makes other people happier and that the world in general is immensely a gainer by it. Utilitarianism, therefore, could only attain its end by the general cultivation of nobleness of character, even if each individual were only benefited by the nobleness of others, and his own, so far as happiness is concerned, were a sheer deduction from the benefit. But the bare enunciation of such an absurdity as this last, renders refutation superfluous.

According to the greatest happiness principle, as above explained, the ultimate end, with reference to and for the sake of which all other things are desirable (whether we are considering our own good or that of other people), is an existence exempt as far as possible from pain, and as rich as possible in enjoyments, both in point of quantity and quality; the test of quality, and the rule for measuring it against quantity, being the preference felt by those who, in their opportunities of experience, to which must be added their habits of self-consciousness and self-observation, are best furnished with the means of comparison. This, being according to the utilitarian opinion the end of human action, is necessarily also the standard of morality; which may accordingly be defined [as] the rules and precepts for human conduct, by the observance of which an existence such as has been described might be, to the greatest extent possible, secured to all mankind; and not to them only, but, so far as the nature of things admits, to the whole sentient creation. . . .

I must again repeat what the assailants of utilitarianism seldom have the justice to acknowledge, that the happiness which forms the utilitarian standard of what is right in conduct, is not the agent's own happiness, but that of all concerned. As between his own happiness and that of others, utilitarianism requires him to be as strictly impartial as a disinterested and benevolent spectator. In the golden rule of Jesus of Nazareth, we read the complete spirit of the ethics of utility. To do as one would be done by,[4] and to love one's neighbour as oneself,[5] constitute the ideal perfection of utilitarian morality. As the means of making the nearest approach to this ideal, utility would enjoin, first, that laws and social arrangements should place the happiness, or (as speaking practically it may be called) the interest, of every individual, as nearly as possible in harmony with the interest of the whole; and secondly, that education and opinion, which have so vast a power over human character, should so use that power as to establish in the mind of every individual an indissoluble association between his own happiness and the good of the whole; especially between his own happiness and the practice of such modes of conduct, negative and positive, as regard for the universal happiness prescribes: so that not only he may be unable to conceive the possibility of happiness to himself consistently with conduct opposed to the general good, but also that a direct impulse to promote the general good may be in every individual one of the habitual motives of action, and the sentiments connected therewith may fill a large and prominent place in every human being's sentient existence. If the impugners of the utilitarian morality represented it to their own minds in this its true character, I know not what recommendation possessed by any other morality they could possibly affirm to be wanting to it; what more beautiful or more exalted developments of human nature any other ethical system can be supposed to foster, or what springs of action, not accessible to the utilitarian, such systems rely on for giving effect to their mandates.

The objectors to utilitarianism cannot always be charged with representing it in a discreditable light. On the contrary, those among them who entertain anything like a just idea of its disinterested character sometimes find fault with its standard as being too high for humanity. They say it is exacting too much to require that people shall always act from the inducement of promoting the general interests of society. But this is to mistake the very meaning of a standard of morals and to confound the rule of action with the motive of it. It is the business of ethics to tell us what are our duties, or by what test we may know them; but no system of ethics requires that the sole motive of all we do shall be a feeling of duty; on the contrary, ninety-nine hundredths of all our actions are done from other motives, and rightly so done, if the rule of duty does not condemn them. It is the more unjust to utilitarianism that this particular misapprehension should be made a ground of objection to it, inasmuch as utilitarian moralists have gone beyond almost all others in affirming that the motive has nothing to do with the morality of the action, though much with the worth of the agent. He who saves a fellow creature from drowning does what is morally right, whether his motive be duty, or the hope of being paid for his trouble; he who betrays the friend that trusts him, is guilty of a crime, even if his object be to serve another friend to whom he is under greater obligations.

But to speak only of actions done from the motive of duty and in direct obedience to principle: it is a misapprehension of the utilitarian mode of thought, to conceive it as implying that people should fix their minds upon so wide a generality as the world, or society at large. The great majority of good actions are intended, not for the benefit of the world, but for that of individuals, of which the good of the world is made up; and the thoughts of the most virtuous man need not on these occasions travel beyond the particular persons concerned, except so far as is necessary to assure himself that in benefiting them he is not violating the rights—that is, the legitimate and authorized expectations—of anyone else. The multiplication of happiness is, according to the utilitarian ethics, the object of virtue: the occasions on which any person (except one in a thousand) has it in his power to do this on an extended scale, in other words, to be a public benefactor, are but exceptional; and on these occasions alone is he called on to consider public utility; in every other case, private utility, the interest or happiness of some few persons, is all he has to attend to. Those alone the influence of whose actions extends to society in general, need concern themselves habitually about so large an object. In the case of abstinences indeed—of things which people forbear to do, from moral considerations, though the consequences in the particular case might be beneficial—it would be unworthy of an intelligent agent not to be consciously aware that the action is of a class which, if practised generally, would be generally injurious, and that this is the ground of the obligation to abstain from it. The amount of regard for the public interest implied in this recognition is no greater than is demanded by every system of morals, for they all enjoin to abstain from whatever is manifestly pernicious to society. . . .

We not uncommonly hear the doctrine of utility inveighed against as a *godless* doctrine. If it be necessary to say anything at all against so mere an assumption, we may say that the question depends upon what idea we have formed of the moral character of the Deity. If it be a true belief that God desires, above all things, the happiness of his creatures, and that this was his purpose in their creation, utility is not only not a godless doctrine, but more profoundly religious than any other. If it be meant that utilitarianism does not recognise the revealed will of God as the supreme law of morals, I answer that a utilitarian who believes in the perfect goodness and wisdom of God necessarily believes that whatever God has thought fit to reveal on the subject of morals, must fulfil the requirements of utility in a supreme degree. . . .

Again, defenders of utility often find themselves called upon to reply to such objections as this—that there is not time, previous to action, for calculating and weighing the effects of any line of conduct on the general happiness. This is exactly as if anyone were to say that it is impossible to guide our conduct by Christianity because there is not time, on every occasion on which anything has to be done, to read through the Old and New Testaments. The answer to the objection is that there has been ample time, namely, the whole past duration of the human species. During all that time mankind have been learning by experience the tendencies of actions, on which experience all the prudence, as well as all the morality of life, is dependent. People talk as if the commencement of this course of experience had hitherto been put off, and as if, at the moment when some man feels tempted to meddle with the property or life of another, he had to begin considering for the first time whether murder and theft are injurious to human happiness. Even then I do not think that he would find the question very puzzling; but, at all events, the matter is now done to his hand. It is truly a whimsical supposition that if mankind were agreed to considering utility to be the test of morality, they would remain without any agreement as to what is useful, and would take no measures for having their notions on the subject taught to the young and enforced by law and opinion. There is no difficulty in proving any ethical standard whatever to work ill, if we suppose universal idiocy to be conjoined with it; but on any hypothesis short of that, mankind must by this time have acquired positive beliefs as to the effects of some actions on their happiness; and [the] beliefs which have thus come down are the rules of morality for the multitude, and for the philosopher until he has succeeded in finding better. . . .

Chapter IV: Of What Sort of Proof the Principle of Utility Is Susceptible

. . . Questions of ultimate ends do not admit of proof, in the ordinary acceptation of the term. To be incapable of proof by reasoning is common to all first principles; to the first premises of our knowledge, as well as to those of our conduct. But the former, being matters of fact, may be the subject of a direct appeal to the faculties which judge of fact—namely, our senses and our internal consciousness. Can an appeal be made to the same faculties on questions of practical ends? Or by what other faculty is cognizance taken of them?

Questions about ends are, in other words, questions what things are desirable. The utilitarian doctrine is that happiness is desirable, and the only thing desirable, as an end; all other things being only desirable as means to that end. What ought to be required of this doctrine—what conditions is it requisite that the doctrine should fulfil—to make good its claim to be believed?

The only proof capable of being given that an object is visible, is that people actually see it. The only proof that a sound is audible, is that people hear it: and so of the other sources of our experience. In like manner, I apprehend, the sole evidence it is possible to produce that anything is desirable, is that people do actually desire it. If the end which the utilitarian doctrine proposes to itself were not, in theory and in practice, acknowledged to be an end, nothing could ever convince any person that it was so. No reason can be given why the general happiness is desirable, except that each person, so far as he believes it to be attainable, desires his own happiness. This, however, being a fact, we have not only all the proof which the case admits of, but all which it is possible to require, that happiness is a good: that each person's happiness is a good to that person, and the general happiness, therefore, a good to the aggregate of all persons. Happiness has made out its title as *one* of the ends of conduct, and consequently one of the criteria of morality.

But it has not, by this alone, proved itself to be the sole criterion. To do that, it would seem, by the same rule, necessary to show not only that people desire happiness, but that they never desire anything else. Now it is palpable that they do desire things which, in common language, are decidedly distinguished from happiness. They desire, for example, virtue and the absence of vice, no less really than pleasure and the absence of pain. The desire of virtue is not as universal, but it is as authentic a fact, as the desire of happiness. And hence the opponents of the utilitarian standard deem that they have a right to infer that there are other ends of human action besides happiness, and that happiness is not the standard of approbation and disapprobation.

But does the utilitarian doctrine deny that people desire virtue, or maintain that virtue is not a thing to be desired? The very reverse. It maintains not only that virtue is to be desired, but that it is to be desired disinterestedly, for itself. Whatever may be the opinion of utilitarian moralists as to the original conditions by which virtue is made virtue; however they may believe (as they do) that actions and dispositions are only virtuous because they promote another end than virtue; yet this being granted, and it having been decided, from considerations of this description, what *is* virtuous, they not only place virtue at the very head of the things which are good as means to the ultimate end, but they also recognise as a psychological fact the possibility of its being, to the individual, a good in itself, without looking to any end beyond it; and hold that the mind is not in a right state, not in a state conformable to utility, not in the state most conducive to the general happiness, unless it does love virtue in this manner—as a thing desirable in itself, even although, in the individual instance, it should not produce those other desirable consequences which it tends to produce, and on account of which it is held to be virtue. This opinion is not, in the smallest degree, a departure from the happiness principle. The ingredients of happiness are very various and each of them is desirable in itself, and not merely when considered as swelling an aggregate. The principle of utility does not mean that any given pleasure, as music, for instance, or any given exemption from pain, as for example health, are to be looked upon as means to a collective something termed happiness, and to be desired on that account. They are desired and desirable in and for themselves; besides being means, they are a part of the end. Virtue, according to the utilitarian doctrine, is not naturally and originally part of the end, but it is capable of becoming so; and in those who love it disinterestedly it has become so, and is desired and cherished, not as a means to happiness, but as a part of their happiness. . . .

We have now, then, an answer to the question, of what sort of proof the principle of utility is susceptible. If the opinion which I have now stated is psychologically true—if human nature is so constituted as to desire nothing which is not either a part of happiness or a means of happiness, we can have no other proof, and we require no other, that these are the only things desirable. If so, happiness is the sole end of human action, and the promotion of it the test by which to judge of all human conduct; from whence it necessarily follows that it must be the criterion of morality, since a part is included in the whole.

And now to decide whether this is really so; whether mankind do desire nothing for itself but that which is a pleasure to them, or of which the absence is a pain; we have evidently arrived at a question of fact and experience, dependent, like all similar questions, upon evidence. It can only be determined by practised self-consciousness and self-observation, assisted by observation of others. I believe that these sources of evidence, impartially consulted, will declare that desiring a thing and finding it pleasant, aversion to it and thinking of it as painful, are phenomena entirely inseparable, or rather two parts of the same phenomenon; in strictness of language, two different modes of naming the same psychological fact: that to think of an object as desirable (unless for the sake of its consequences), and to think of it as pleasant, are one and the same thing; and that to desire anything, except in proportion as the idea of it is pleasant, is a physical and metaphysical impossibility.

▶ NOTES

1. Epicurus (341–270 B.C.E.) was a Greek philosopher. [D.C.A., ed.]
2. Stoicism is the school of philosophy founded by the Greek philosopher Zeno of Citium (about 335–263 B.C.E). [D.C.A.]
3. Mill refers here primarily to Jeremy Bentham (1748–1832), the English jurist and philosopher who first proposed the theory of utilitarianism. [D.C.A.]
4. Matthew 7:21; Luke 6:31 [D.C.A.]
5. Matthew 22:39 [D.C.A.]

Fundamental Principles of the Metaphysics of Morals

Immanuel Kant

Immanuel Kant was born in 1724 in Königsberg, Prussia, where he spent his entire life. As a boy he attended the Collegium Fridericanum, a school run by the Pietists (the Lutheran sect to which his family belonged). In 1740 he enrolled in the University of Königsberg, where he studied a wide variety of subjects, including theology, philosophy, mathematics, physics, and medicine. He withdrew from the university in 1747 to support himself by working as a private tutor for families in the Königsberg area. He resumed his studies in 1754 and completed his degree the following year. He then became a lecturer at the University of Königsberg, teaching such diverse subjects as mathematics, geography, mineralogy, and philosophy. Fifteen years later he was appointed Professor of Logic and Metaphysics. His writings—especially his monumental *Critique of Pure Reason* (1781)—brought him increasing fame, and students came from afar to hear him lecture. In 1797 he stopped lecturing but continued to write. He died in Königsberg in 1804 at the age of seventy-nine.

Kant's principal works, in addition to the *Critique of Pure Reason,* are *Prolegomena to Any Future Metaphysics* (1783), *Fundamental Principles of the Metaphysics of Morals* (1785), *Critique of Practical Reason* (1788), and *Critique of Judgment* (1790).

Our selection is taken from *Fundamental Principles of the Metaphysics of Morals,* a work whose aim, Kant explains in his preface, is "to seek out and establish the supreme principle of morality." According to Kant, the moral worth of an action is determined by one's motive, not by the consequences of the action. And the proper motive (what makes a will a *good* will) is to do one's duty simply because it is one's duty. To act out of duty means to act out of respect for the law, and to act out of respect for the law means to follow the "categorical imperative." This imperative states that our action should be "universalizable"—which means that the personal policy (maxim) on which our action is based must be one that we could consistently will that all persons follow. If our maxim cannot be universalized, the action is immoral. For example, the maxim of making a false promise to escape a difficulty cannot consistently be universalized because, if everyone followed it, promises would no longer be able to function as promises because no one would believe them. The categorical imperative is, for Kant, the ultimate criterion for determining the morality of any action.

According to Kant, the categorical imperative can be expressed in various equivalent ways, including the injunction that we should always treat persons (including ourselves) as ends in themselves, and never simply as means to an end. Returning to his example of making a false promise, he explains that such a promise is immoral because it uses the person lied to merely as means to obtain one's end.

▼

First Section: Transition from the Common Rational Knowledge of Morality to the Philosophical

Nothing can possibly be conceived in the world, or even out of it, which can be called good without qualification, except a *good will*. Intelligence, wit, judgment, and the other talents of the mind, however they may be named, or courage, resolution, perseverance, as qualities of temperament, are undoubtedly good and desirable in many respects; but these gifts of nature may also become extremely bad and mischievous if the will which is to make use of them, and which, therefore, constitutes what is called *character*, is not good. It is the same with the gifts of fortune. Power, riches, honour, even health, and the general well-being and contentment with one's condition which is called *happiness*, inspire pride, and often presumption, if there is not a good will to correct the influence of these on the mind, and with this also to rectify the whole principle of acting and adapt it to its end. The sight of a being who is not adorned with a single feature of a pure and good will, enjoying unbroken prosperity, can never give pleasure to an impartial rational spectator. Thus a good will appears to constitute the indispensable condition even of being worthy of happiness.

There are even some qualities which are of service to this good will itself and may facilitate its action, yet which have no intrinsic unconditional value, but always presuppose a good will, and this qualifies the esteem that we justly have for them and does not permit us to regard them as absolutely good. Moderation in the affections and passions, self-control, and calm deliberation are not only good in many respects, but even seem to constitute part of the intrinsic worth of the person; but they are far from deserving to be called good without qualification, although they have been so unconditionally praised by the ancients. For without the principles of a good will, they may become extremely bad; and the coolness of a villain not only makes him far more dangerous, but also directly makes him more abominable in our eyes than he would have been without it.

A good will is good not because of what it performs or effects, not by its aptness for the attainment of some proposed end, but simply by virtue of the volition; that is, it is good in itself, and considered by itself is to be esteemed much higher than all that can be brought about by it in favour of any inclination, nay, even of the sum total of all inclinations. Even if it should happen that, owing to special disfavour of fortune, or the [stingy] provision of a stepmotherly nature, this will should wholly lack power to accomplish its purpose; if with its greatest efforts it should yet achieve nothing, and there should remain only the good will (not, to be sure, a mere wish, but the summoning of all means in our power); then, like a jewel, it would still shine by its own light, as a thing which has its whole value in itself. Its usefulness or fruitlessness can neither add to nor take away anything from this value. It would be, as it were, only the setting to enable us to handle it the more conveniently in common commerce or to attract to it the attention of those who are not yet connoisseurs, but not to recommend it to true connoisseurs or to determine its value. . . .

We have, then, to develop the notion of a will which deserves to be highly esteemed for itself and is good without a view to anything further, a notion which exists already in the sound natural understanding, requiring rather to be cleared up than to be taught, and which in estimating the value of our actions always takes the first place and constitutes the condition of all the rest. In order to do this, we will take the notion of *duty*, which includes that of a good will, although implying certain subjective restrictions and hindrances. These, however, far from concealing it or rendering it unrecognizable, rather bring it out by contrast and make it shine forth so much the brighter.

I omit here all actions which are already recognized as inconsistent with duty, although they may be useful for this or that purpose, for with these the question whether they are done *from duty* cannot arise at all, since they even conflict with it. I also set aside those actions which really conform to duty, but to which men have *no direct inclination,* performing them because they are impelled to it by some other inclination. For in this case we can readily distinguish whether the action which agrees with duty is done from duty or from a selfish view. It is much harder to make this distinction when the action accords with duty, and the subject has besides a *direct* inclination to it. For example, it is always a matter of duty that a dealer should not overcharge an inexperienced purchaser; and wherever there is much commerce the prudent tradesman does not overcharge, but keeps a fixed price for everyone, so that a child buys of him as well as any other. Men are thus honestly served; but this is not enough to make us believe that the tradesman has so acted from duty and from principles of honesty: his own advantage required it. It is out of the question in this case to suppose that he might besides have a direct inclination in favour of the buyers, so that, as it were, from love he should give no advantage to one over another. Accordingly, the action was done neither from duty nor from direct inclination, but merely with a selfish view.

On the other hand, it is a duty to maintain one's life; and, in addition, everyone has also a direct inclination to do so. But on this account the often anxious care which most men take for it has no intrinsic worth, and their maxim[1] has no moral import. They preserve their life *as duty requires,* no doubt, but not *because duty requires.* On the other hand, if adversity and hopeless sorrow have completely taken away the relish for life; if the unfortunate one, strong in mind, indignant at his fate rather than desponding or dejected, wishes for death, and yet preserves his life without loving it—not from inclination or fear, but from duty—then his maxim has a moral worth.

To be beneficent when we can is a duty; and besides this, there are many minds so sympathetically constituted that, without any other motive of vanity or self-interest, they find a pleasure in spreading joy around them and can take delight in the satisfaction of others so far as it is their own work. But I maintain that in such a case an action of this kind, however proper, however amiable it may be, has nevertheless no true moral worth, but is on a level with other inclinations, e.g., the inclination to honour, which, if it is happily directed to that which is in fact of public utility and accordant with duty, and consequently honourable, deserves praise and encouragement, but not esteem. For the maxim lacks the moral import, namely, that such actions be done from duty, not from inclination. Put the case that the mind of that philanthropist was clouded by sorrow of his own, extinguishing all sympathy with the lot of others, and that while he still has the power to benefit others in distress, he is not touched by their trouble because he is absorbed with his own. And now suppose that he tears himself out of this dead insensibility and performs the action without any inclination to it, but simply from duty; then first has his action its genuine moral worth. Further still; if nature has put little sympathy in the heart of this or that man; if he, supposed to be an upright man, is by temperament cold and indifferent to the sufferings of others, perhaps because in respect of his own he is provided with the special gift of patience and fortitude, and supposes, or even requires, that others should have the same—and such a man would certainly not be the meanest product of nature—but if nature had not specially framed him for a philanthropist, would he not still find in himself a source from whence to give himself a far higher worth than that of a good-natured temperament could be? Unquestionably. It is just in this that the moral worth of the character is brought out which is incomparably the highest of all, namely, that he is beneficent, not from inclination, but from duty. . . .

The second proposition[2] is: That an action done from duty derives its moral worth, not from the purpose which is to be attained by it, but from the maxim by which it is determined, and therefore does not depend on the realization of the object of the action, but merely on the *principle of volition* by which the action has taken place, without regard to any object of desire. It is clear from what precedes that the purposes which we may have in view in our actions, or their effects regarded as ends and springs of the will, cannot give to actions any unconditional or moral worth. In what, then, can their worth lie, if it is not to consist in the [relation of the will] to its expected effect? It cannot lie anywhere but in the principle of the will, without regard to the ends which can be attained by the action. For the will stands between its a priori principle, which is formal, and its a posteriori spring, which is material,[3] as between two roads; and as it must be determined by something, it follows that it must be determined by the formal principle of volition when an action is done from duty, in which case every material principle has been withdrawn from it.

The third proposition, which is a consequence of the two preceding, I would express thus: Duty is the necessity of acting from respect for the law. I may have *inclination* for an object as the effect of my proposed action, but I cannot have *respect* for it, just for this reason, that it is an effect and not an [activity] of will. Similarly, I cannot have respect for inclination, whether my own or another's; I can at most, if my own, approve it; if another's, sometimes even love it, that is, look on it as favourable to my own interest. It is only what is connected with my will as a principle, by no means as an effect—what does not subserve my inclination, but overpowers it, or at least, in case of choice, excludes it from its calculation—in other words, simply the law of itself, which can be an object of respect, and hence a command. Now an action done from duty must wholly exclude the influence of inclination, and with it every object of the will, so that nothing remains which can determine the will except objectively the law, and subjectively pure respect for this practical law, and consequently the maxim that I should follow this law even to the thwarting of all my inclinations.

Thus the moral worth of an action does not lie in the effect expected from it, nor in any principle of action which requires to borrow its motive from this expected effect. For all these effects—agreeableness of one's condition, and even the promotion of the happiness of others—could have been also brought about by other causes, so that for this there would have been no need of the will of a rational being; whereas it is in this alone that the supreme and unconditional good can be found. The preeminent good which we call moral can therefore consist in nothing else than *the conception of law* in itself, which certainly is only possible in a rational being, in so far as this conception, and not the expected effect, determines the will. This is a good which is already present in the person who acts accordingly, and we have not to wait for it to appear first in the result.

But what sort of law can that be, the conception of which must determine the will, even without paying any regard to the effect expected from it, in order that this will may be called good absolutely and without qualification? As I have deprived the will of every impulse which could arise to it from [obeying a specific] law, there remains nothing but the universal conformity of its actions to law in general, which alone is to serve the will as a principle, that is, I am never to act otherwise than [in such a way] *that I could also will that my maxim should become a universal law.* Here, now, it is the simple conformity to law in general, without assuming any particular law applicable to certain actions, that serves the will as its principle, and must so serve it, if duty is not to be a vain delusion and a chimerical notion. The common reason of men in its practical judgments perfectly coincides with this and always has in view the principle here suggested. Let the question be, for example: May I when in distress make a promise with the intention not to keep it? I readily distinguish here between the two significations which the question may have: whether it is *prudent,* or whether it is *right,* to make a false promise. The former may undoubtedly often be the case. I see clearly indeed that it is not enough to extricate myself from a present difficulty by means of this subterfuge, but it must be well considered whether there may not [afterwards] spring from this lie much greater inconvenience than that from which I now free myself. And as, with all my supposed cunning, the consequences cannot be so easily foreseen, [and trust in me] once lost may be much more injurious to me than any mischief which I seek to avoid at present, it should be considered whether it would not be more prudent to act herein according to a universal maxim, and to make it a habit to promise nothing except with the intention of keeping it. But it is soon clear to me that such a maxim will still only be based on the fear of consequences. Now it is a wholly different thing to be truthful from duty, and to be so from apprehension of injurious consequences. In the first case, the very notion of the action already implies a law for me; in the second case, I must first look about elsewhere to see what results may be combined with it which would affect myself. For to deviate from the principle of duty is beyond all doubt wicked; but to be unfaithful to my maxim of prudence may often be very advantageous to me, although to abide by it is certainly safer. The shortest way, however, and an unerring one, to discover the answer to this question whether a lying promise is consistent with duty, is to ask myself, Should I be content that my maxim (to extricate myself from difficulty by a false promise) should hold good as a universal law, for myself as well as for others, and should I be able to say to myself, "Every one may make a deceitful promise when he finds himself in a difficulty from which he cannot otherwise extricate himself"? Then I presently become aware that while I can will the lie, I can by no means will that lying should be a universal law. For with such a law there would be no promises at all, since it would be in vain to allege my intention in regard to my future actions to those who would not believe this allegation, or if they overhastily did so, would pay me back in my own coin. Hence my maxim, as soon as it should be made a universal law, would necessarily destroy itself.

I do not, therefore, need any far-reaching penetration to discern what I have to do in order that my will may be morally good. Inexperienced in the course of the world, incapable of being prepared for all its contingencies, I only ask myself: Can you also will that your maxim should be a universal law? If not, then it must be rejected, and that not because of a disadvantage accruing from it to myself or even to others, but because it cannot enter as a principle into a possible universal legislation—and reason extorts from me immediate respect for such legislation. I do not indeed as yet discern on what this respect is based (this the philosopher may inquire), but at least I understand this, that it is an estimation of the worth which far outweighs all worth of what is recommended by inclination, and that the necessity of acting from pure respect for the practical law is what constitutes duty, to which every other motive must give place, because it is the condition of a will being good in itself, and the worth of such a will is above everything. . . .

Second Section: Transition from Popular Moral Philosophy to the Metaphysics of Morals

. . . In this study we may not merely advance by the natural steps from the common moral judgment (in this case, very worthy of respect) to the philosophical, as has been already done, but also from a popular philosophy, which goes no further than it can reach by groping with the help of examples, to metaphysics (which does not allow itself to be checked by anything empirical, and—as it must measure the whole extent of this kind of rational knowledge—goes as far as ideal conceptions, where even examples fail us), we must follow and clearly describe the practical faculty of reason, from the general rules of its determination to the point where the notion of duty springs from it.

Everything in nature works according to laws. Rational beings alone have the faculty of acting according to the *conception* of laws, that is, according to principles; [in other words, they] have a will. Since the deduction of actions from principles requires reason, the will is nothing but practical reason. If reason infallibly determines the will, then the actions of such a being which are recognized as objectively necessary are subjectively necessary also; that is, the will is a faculty to choose only that which reason, independent of inclination, recognizes as practically necessary, that is, as good. But if reason of itself does not sufficiently determine the will; if the latter is subject also to subjective conditions (particular impulses) which do not always coincide with the objective conditions; in a word, if the will does not *in itself* completely accord with reason (which is actually the case with men); then the actions which objectively are recognized as necessary are subjectively contingent, and the determination of such a will according to objective laws is *obligation*. That is to say, the relation of the objective laws to a will that is not thoroughly good is conceived as the determination of the will of a rational being by principles of reason, but which the will from its nature does not of necessity follow.

The conception of an objective principle, in so far as it is obligatory for a will, is called a *command* (of reason), and the formula of the command is called an *imperative*. . . .

Now all imperatives command either *hypothetically* or *categorically*. The former represent the practical necessity of a possible action as means to something else that is willed (or at least which one might possibly will). The categorical imperative would be that which represented an action as necessary of itself without reference to another end, that is, as objectively necessary.

Since every practical law represents a possible action as good, and on this account, for a subject who is practically determinable by reason, necessary; [therefore,] all imperatives are formulas determining an action which is necessary according to the principle of a will good in some respects. Now if the action is good only as a means to something else, then the imperative is *hypothetical;* if it is conceived as good in itself and consequently as being necessarily the principle of a will which of itself conforms to reason, then it is *categorical* . . . .

When I conceive a hypothetical imperative in general, I do not know beforehand what it will contain until I am given the condition. But when I conceive a categorical imperative, I know at once what it contains. For as the imperative contains besides the law only the necessity that the maxim shall conform to this law, while the law contains no conditions restricting it, there remains nothing but the general statement that the maxim of the action should conform to a universal law, and it is this conformity alone that the imperative properly represents as necessary.

There is therefore but one categorical imperative, namely this: *Act only on that maxim whereby you can at the same time will that it should become a universal law.*

Now if all imperatives of duty can be deduced from this one imperative as from their principle, then, although it should remain undecided whether what is called duty is not merely a vain notion, yet at least we shall be able to show what we understand by it and what this notion means.

Since the universality of the law according to which effects are produced constitutes what is properly called *nature* in the most general sense (as to form), that is, the existence of things so far as it is determined by general laws, the imperative of duty may be expressed thus: *Act as if the maxim of your action were to become by your will a universal law of nature.*

We will now enumerate a few duties, adopting the usual division of them into duties to ourselves and to others, and into perfect and imperfect duties.[4]

1. A man reduced to despair by a series of misfortunes feels wearied of life, but is still so far in possession of his reason that he can ask himself whether it would not be contrary to his duty to himself to take his own life. Now he inquires whether the maxim of his action could become a universal law of nature. His maxim is: From self-love I adopt it as a principle to shorten my life when its longer duration is likely to bring more evil than satisfaction. It is asked then simply whether this principle founded on self-love can become a universal law of nature. Now we see at once that a system of nature of which it should be a law to destroy life by means of the very feeling whose special nature it is to impel to the improvement of life would contradict itself, and therefore could not exist as a system of nature; hence that maxim cannot possibly exist as a universal law of nature, and consequently would be wholly inconsistent with the supreme principle of all duty.

2. Another finds himself forced by necessity to borrow money. He knows that he will not be able to repay it, but sees also that nothing will be lent to him unless he promises stoutly to repay it in a definite time. He desires to make this promise, but he has still so much conscience as to ask himself: Is it not unlawful and inconsistent with duty to get out of a difficulty in this way? Suppose, however, that he resolves to do so, then the maxim of his action would be expressed thus: When I think myself in want of money, I will borrow money and promise to repay it, although I know that I never can do so. Now this principle of self-love or of one's own advantage may perhaps be consistent with my whole future welfare; but the question now is, Is it right? I change then the suggestion of self-love into a universal law, and state the question thus: How would it be if my maxim were a universal law? Then I see at once that it could never hold as a universal law of nature, but would necessarily contradict itself. For supposing it to be a universal law that everyone, when he thinks himself in a difficulty, should be able to promise whatever he pleases, with the purpose of not keeping his promise; the promise itself would become impossible, as well as the end that one might have in view in it, since no one would consider that anything was promised to him, but would ridicule all such statements as vain pretences.

3. A third finds in himself a talent which, with the help of [cultivation] might make him a useful man in many respects. But he finds himself in comfortable circumstances and prefers to indulge in pleasure rather than to take pains in enlarging and improving his happy natural capacities. He asks, however, whether his maxim of neglect of his natural gifts, besides agreeing with his inclination to indulgence, agrees also with what is called duty. He sees then that a system of nature could indeed subsist with such a universal law although men (like the South Sea islanders) should let their talents rest, and resolve to devote their lives merely to idleness, amusement, and propagation of their species—in a word, to enjoyment; but he cannot possibly *will* that this should be a universal law of nature, or be implanted in us as such by a natural instinct. For, as a rational being, he necessarily wills that his faculties be developed, since they serve him and have been given him for all sorts of possible purposes.

4. A fourth, who is in prosperity, while he sees that others have to contend with great wretchedness and that he could help them, thinks: What concern is it of mine? Let everyone be as happy as heaven pleases, or as he can make himself; I will take nothing from him nor even envy him, only I do not wish to contribute anything to his welfare or to his assistance in distress. Now no doubt if such a mode of thinking were a universal law, the human race might very well subsist, and doubtless even better than in a state in which everyone talks of sympathy and good will, or even takes care occasionally to put it into practice, but, on the other side, also cheats when he can, betrays the rights of men, or otherwise violates them. But although it is possible that a universal law of nature might exist in accordance with that maxim, it is impossible to will that such a principle should have the universal validity of a law of nature. For a will which resolved this would contradict itself, inasmuch as many cases might occur in which one would have need of the love and sympathy of others, and in which, by such a law of nature, sprung from his own will, he would deprive himself of all hope of the aid he desires.

These are a few of the many actual duties, or at least what we regard as such, which obviously fall into two classes on the one principle that we have laid down. We must be *able to will* that a maxim of our action should be a universal law. This is the canon of the moral appreciation of the action generally. Some actions are of such a character that their maxim cannot without contradiction be even *conceived* as a universal law of nature, far from it being possible that we should will that it should be so. In others this intrinsic impossibility is not found, but still it is impossible to will that their maxim should be raised to the universality of a law of nature, since such a will would contradict itself. It is easily seen that the former violate strict or rigorous (inflexible) duty; the latter only laxer (meritorious) duty. Thus it has been completely shown by these examples how all duties depend as regards the nature of the obligation (not the object of the action) on the same principle. . . .

. . . Man, and generally any rational being, exists as an end in himself, not merely as a means to be arbitrarily used by this or that will, but in all his actions, whether they concern himself or other rational beings, must be always regarded at the same time as an end. All objects of the inclinations have only a conditional worth; for if the inclinations and the wants founded on them did not exist, then their object would be without value. But the inclinations themselves, being sources of want, are so far from having an absolute worth for which they should be desired, that, on the contrary, it must be the universal wish of every rational being to be wholly free from them. Thus the worth of any object which is to be acquired by our action is always conditional. Beings whose existence depends not on our will but on nature's, have nevertheless, if they are nonrational beings, only a relative value as means, and are therefore called *things*. Rational beings, on the contrary, are called *persons* because their very nature points them out as ends in themselves, that is, as something which must not be used merely as means, and so far therefore restricts freedom of action (and is an object of respect). These, therefore, are not merely *subjective* ends, whose existence has a worth *for us* as an effect of our action, but *objective* ends, that is, things whose existence is an end *in itself*. [This kind of end is one] for which no other can be substituted, which they should subserve merely as means; for otherwise nothing whatever would possess absolute worth. But if all worth were conditioned and therefore contingent, then there would be no supreme practical principle of reason whatever.

If, then, there is a supreme practical principle or, in respect of the human will, a categorical imperative, it must be one which, being drawn from the conception of that which is necessarily an end for everyone because it is an end in itself, constitutes an *objective* principle of will, and can therefore serve as a universal practical law. The foundation of this principle is: *Rational nature exists as an end in itself*. Man necessarily conceives his own existence as being so: so far, then, this is a *subjective* principle of human actions. But every other rational being regards its existence similarly, just on the same rational principle that holds for me; so that it is at the same time an objective principle, from which as a supreme practical law all laws of the will must be capable of being deduced. Accordingly, the practical imperative will be as follows: *So act as to treat humanity, whether in your own person or in that of any other, in every case as an end, never as a means only.* We will now inquire whether this can be practically carried out.

[Let us return to] the previous examples.

First, under the head of necessary duty to oneself: He who contemplates suicide should ask himself whether his action can be consistent with the idea of humanity as an end in itself. If he destroys himself in order to escape from painful circumstances, he uses a person merely as a means to maintain a tolerable condition up to the end of life. But a man is not a thing, that is to say, something which can be used merely as means, but must in all his actions be always considered as an end in himself. I cannot, therefore, dispose in any way of a man in my own person so as to mutilate him, to damage or kill him. . . .

Secondly, as regards necessary duties, or those of strict obligation, towards others: He who is thinking of making a lying promise to others will see at once that he would be using another man merely as a means, without the latter containing at the same time the end in himself. For he whom I propose by such a promise to use for my own purposes cannot possibly assent to my mode of acting towards him, and therefore cannot himself contain the end of this action. This violation of the principle of humanity in other men is more obvious if we take in examples of attacks on the freedom and property of others. For then it is clear that he who transgresses the rights of men intends to use the person of others merely as means, without considering that as rational beings they ought always to be esteemed also as ends, that is, as beings who must be capable of containing in themselves the end of the very same action.

Thirdly, as regards contingent (meritorious) duties to oneself: It is not enough that the action does not violate humanity in our own person as an end in itself; it must also *harmonize* with it. Now there are in humanity capacities of greater perfection which belong to the end that nature has in view in regard to humanity in ourselves as the subject: to neglect these might perhaps be consistent with the *maintenance* of humanity as an end in itself, but not with the *advancement* of this end.

Fourthly, as regards meritorious duties towards others: The natural end which all men have is their own happiness. Now humanity might indeed subsist although no one should contribute anything to the happiness of others, provided he did not intentionally withdraw anything from it; but after all, this would only harmonize negatively, not positively, with humanity as an end in itself, if everyone does not also endeavour, as far as in him lies, to forward the ends of others. For the ends of any subject that is an end in himself, ought as far as possible to be my ends also, if that conception is to have its full effect with me.

▶ NOTES

1. *maxim:* the personal policy on which a person acts. In the case described here, the maxim would be to follow one's inclination to preserve one's life. Kant later contrasts a maxim with *universal law,* which binds all rational creatures. A maxim is *subjective* principle, while universal law is an *objective* principle. [D.C.A., ed.]

2. The first proposition [not identified as such by Kant] was that to have moral worth an action must be done from duty. [T.K.A., trans.]

3. *A priori* means "independent of experience" (literally, in Latin, "from what comes earlier"); *a posteriori* means "dependent on experience" ("from what comes later"). Duty is an a priori principle of the will be-

cause it binds prior to any experience; the incentive ("spring") of action is a posteriori because it depends on the person's experience. Kant here draws a further contrast between duty and incentive: Duty is a *formal* principle because it refers to the general form any action should take; incentive is *material* because it involves the situation ("matter") of a particular action. [D.C.A.]

4. In Kant's terminology, a *perfect duty* is one that prohibits a specific action, while an *imperfect duty* commands us to achieve some general goal without specifying what means we are to use. Kant's following four examples illustrate, respectively, (1) a perfect duty to ourselves (not to commit suicide), (2) a perfect duty to others (not to make false promises), (3) an imperfect duty to ourselves (to develop our talents), and (4) an imperfect duty to others (to help those in need). [D.C.A.]

Nicomachean Ethics

Aristotle

Aristotle was born in the town of Stagira in northern Greece in 384 B.C.E. At the age of seventeen, he went to Athens to study at Plato's Academy, where he remained until Plato's death twenty years later. He then spent three years in the city of Assos in Asia Minor and two years in Mytilene on the island of Lesbos. In 343 or 342, he accepted the invitation of King Philip II of Macedon to become the tutor of his thirteen-year-old son, Alexander (later known as Alexander the Great). After a few years at the royal court in Pella, Aristotle returned to Stagira. In 335 he went back to Athens, where he founded a school called the Lyceum. When Alexander died in 323, strong anti-Macedonian sentiment arose in Athens. Because of his connections with Macedon, Aristotle thought it prudent to leave Athens. He went to Chalcis on the island of Euboea, where he died the following year of a stomach ailment.

Aristotle is the author of two very different kinds of philosophical writings: polished works, intended for the general reading public, and notes from which he lectured, intended for circulation among his students and associates. The polished works have been entirely lost except for a few fragments; what has survived are the notes from his lectures on a wide variety of topics, including logic, biology, physics, psychology, metaphysics, and ethics.

Our selection is taken from the first two books of the set of notes known as the *Nicomachean Ethics*. Here Aristotle argues that the ultimate goal everyone seeks is happiness and that being moral is a necessary part of a happy life. Happiness, Aristotle contends, consists in living rationally. Living rationally requires that two parts of a person's soul function well: the intellectual (strictly rational) part and the part containing emotions and desires (while emotions and desires are not in themselves rational, they can obey reason).

These two parts of the soul function well if they possess their proper virtues (excellences, good inner dispositions). *Intellectual virtues* are those qualities that enable the strictly rational part of the soul to carry out its function; *moral virtues* (virtues of character) are those qualities that enable emotions and desires to fulfill their proper functions. Aristotle argues that a person who lives in accordance with the intellectual and moral virtues attains happiness and is moral.

Intellectual virtues include such qualities as wisdom and intelligence; moral virtues include such traits as courage and temperance (self-control). Aristotle defines moral virtue as a state of character that aims at the mean between extremes—the extremes of having an excess or a deficiency of emotion or desire. Both excess and deficiency are vices; virtue lies in the middle. For example, regarding the emotion of confidence, foolhardiness and cowardice are vices and courage is the virtue. Aristotle explains that the way to acquire a moral virtue is to perform repeatedly the appropriate acts; to become a temperate person, for example, one must frequently exercise acts of self-control.

▼

The Nicomachean Ethics of Aristotle, trans. J. E. C. Welldon. New York: Macmillan, 1892 (updated stylistically).

Book I

Chapter 1[1]

Every art and every scientific inquiry, and similarly every action and purpose, may be said to aim at some good. Hence the good has been well defined as that at which all things aim. But it is clear that there is a difference in the ends;[2] for some ends are activities, and others are products beyond the mere activities. Also, where there are certain ends beyond the actions, the products are naturally superior to the activities.

Since there are various actions, arts, and sciences, the ends are also various. Thus the end of medicine is health; of shipbuilding, a vessel; of strategy, victory; and of household management, wealth. It often happens that a number of such arts or sciences that fall under a single science, as the art of bridle-making and all the other arts concerning the equipment of horses fall under horsemanship, and as every military action falls under strategy. And in the same way other arts or sciences fall under other faculties. But in all these cases the ends of the master arts or sciences, whatever they may be, are more desirable than those of the subordinate arts or sciences, since it is for the sake of the former that the latter are sought. It makes no difference to the argument whether the activities themselves are the ends of the actions, or something else beyond the activities, as in the above-mentioned sciences.

Chapter 2

If it is true that in the sphere of action there is an end that we wish for its own sake, and for the sake of which we wish everything else, and that we do not desire all things for the sake of something else (if that is so, the process would go on to infinity and our desire will be empty and futile), it is clear that this will be the good, namely the supreme good. Does it not follow that the knowledge of this supreme good is of great importance for the conduct of life, and that, if we know it, we will be like archers who have a target to aim at, and will have a better chance of attaining what we want?

If this is the case, we must try to comprehend, at least in outline, the nature of the supreme good and the science to which it belongs. It would seem to belong to the most authoritative science, the master science; and this science is politics.[3] For politics is what determines what sciences are necessary in states, and what kind of sciences should be learned, and how far they should be learned by particular people. We perceive too that the sciences that are held in the highest esteem—for example, strategy, household management, and rhetoric—are subordinate to politics. But since it makes use of the other practical sciences, and also legislates things to be done and to be left undone, it follows that its end will include the ends of all the other sciences, and will therefore be the true good of human beings. For although the good of an individual is the same as the good of a state, the good of the state, whether in attainment or in preservation, is evidently greater and more perfect. For while in an individual by himself it is something to be thankful for, it is nobler and more divine in a nation or state. These then are the objects at which the present inquiry aims, and it is in a sense a political inquiry.

Chapter 3

Our statement of these matters will be adequate if it is made with all the clearness that the subject matter admits, for it would be as wrong to expect the same degree of accuracy in all kinds of discourse as it would be to expect it in all manufactured items. Things noble and just, which are the subjects of investigation in politics, exhibit so great a diversity and uncertainty that they are sometimes thought to have only a conventional, and not a natural, existence. There is the same sort of uncertainty in regard to good things, since injuries often result from them; thus there have been cases in which people were ruined by wealth or by courage. Since our subjects and our premises are of this nature, we must be content to indicate the truth roughly and in outline; and since our subjects and premises are true generally but not universally, we must be content to arrive at conclusions that are only generally true. It is right to receive particular statements in the same spirit; for an educated person will expect accuracy in each subject only to the extent that the nature of the subject allows. One might as well accept probable reasoning from a mathematician as require demonstrative proofs from a rhetorician. . . .

Chapter 4

Since every kind of knowledge and every moral purpose aims at some good, what in our view is the good at which politics aims, and what is the highest of all goods achievable by action? With regard to its name, there is a general agreement: The masses and the cultured classes agree in calling it happiness, and conceive that "to live well" or "to do well" is the same thing as "to be happy." But they do not agree regarding the nature of happiness, nor do the masses give the same account of it as the philosophers. The former define it as something visible and palpable, such as pleasure, wealth, or honor; different people give different definitions of it; and often the same person gives different definitions at different times. When a person has been ill, happiness is health; when he is poor, it is wealth; and if he is conscious of his own ignorance, he envies people who use grand language above his own comprehension. Some philosophers, on the other hand, have held that, besides these various goods, there is an absolute good that is the cause of goodness in them all.[4] It would perhaps be a waste of time to examine all these opinions; it will be enough to examine the most popular ones, or those that seem more or less reasonable. . . .

Chapter 5

. . . It seems reasonable to derive men's conception of the good or of happiness from their lives. Ordinary or vulgar people conceive it to be pleasure, and accordingly approve a life of enjoyment. For there are three prominent lives: the life of pleasure, the political life, and, thirdly, the contemplative life. The mass of men show themselves to be completely slavish, choosing the life of cattle, but they get a hearing because so many persons in authority share the tastes of Sardanapallus.[5] Cultivated and practical people, on the other hand, identify happiness with honor, since honor is the general end of political life. But this appears too superficial for our present purpose, for honor seems to depend more on the people who pay it than on the person to whom it is paid, and we have an intuitive feeling that the good is something that is proper to a man himself and cannot easily be taken away from him. It seems too that the reason why men seek honor is to be confident of their own goodness. Accordingly they seek it from the wise and those who know them well, and they seek it on the ground of virtue—and so it is clear that, in their judgment at least, virtue is superior to honor. It would perhaps be right then to look upon virtue rather than honor as being the end of the political life. And virtue, it appears, lacks completeness; for it seems that a man can possess virtue and yet be asleep or inactive throughout life. Moreover, he may experience the greatest calamities and misfortunes. But no one would call such a life a life of happiness, unless he were maintaining a paradox. It is not necessary to dwell further on this subject, since it is sufficiently discussed in popular philosophical treatises. The third life is the contemplative, which we will investigate later on.[6]

The life of money-making is in a sense a life of constraint, and it is clear that wealth is not the good we are looking for, since money is merely useful, as means to something else. It would be a more reasonable view therefore that the things mentioned before[7] are ends, since they are valued for their own sake. Yet they too are apparently not the good, though much argument has been employed to show that they are. We may now dismiss this subject. . . .

Chapter 7

Let us return to the good that we are seeking and consider what its nature may be. For it is clearly different in different actions or arts: It is one thing in medicine, another in strategy, and so on. What then is the good in each of these instances? It is presumably that for the sake of which all else is done. In medicine this is health; in strategy, victory; in domestic architecture, a house; and so on. But in every action and purpose it is the end, for it is for the sake of the end that people do everything else. If, then, there is a certain end of all action, it will be this that is the good attainable by action; and if there are several such ends, it will be these.

Our argument has arrived by a different path at the same conclusion as before, but we must try to elucidate it still further. There seem to be several ends, and since we desire some of these—for example, wealth, flutes, and instruments generally—as means to something else, it is evident that they are not all final ends. But the highest good is clearly something final. Hence if there is only one final end, this will be the object that we are seeking; and if there are more than one, it will be the most final of them. We speak of that which is sought after for its own sake as more final than that which is sought after as a means to something else; we speak of that which is never desired as a means to something else as more final than things desired both in themselves and as means to something else; and we speak of a thing as absolutely final if it is always desired in itself and never as a means to something else. It seems that happiness above all answers to this description, since we always desire happiness for its own sake and never as a means to something else, whereas we desire honor, pleasure, intellect, and every virtue partly for their own sakes (for we desire them independently of what might result from them), but partly also for the sake of happiness, because we think that they will be means to happiness. Happiness, on the other hand, no one desires for the sake of these things, nor indeed as a means to anything else at all.

We come to the same conclusion if we start from the consideration of self-sufficiency, if we may assume that the final good is self-sufficient. When we speak of self-sufficiency, we do not mean that a person leads a solitary life all by himself, but that he has parents, children, a wife, friends, and fellow citizens in general, since man is naturally a social being. But here it is necessary to prescribe some limit; for if the circle be extended so as to include parents, descendants, and friends of friends, it will go on indefinitely. Leaving this point, however, for future investigation, we define the self-sufficient as that which, taken by itself, makes life desirable and lacking in nothing. And this is our conception of happiness.

We conceive happiness to be the most desirable of all things, and not merely as one among other good things. If it were one among other good things, the addition of the smallest good would increase its desirableness; for the addition would make it a greater good, and the greater of two goods is always the more desirable. It appears, then, that happiness is something final and self-sufficient, the end of all action.

Perhaps, however, it seems to be a platitude to say that happiness is the supreme good; what we need to do is to define its nature more clearly. The best way to arrive at such a definition is probably to ascertain the function of a human being. For, as with a flute player, a sculptor, or any artisan, or in fact anyone who has a definite function and action, his goodness seems to lie in his function, so it would seem to be with man, if indeed man has a definite function. Can we say that while a carpenter and a shoemaker have definite functions and actions, man, unlike them, is naturally functionless? The reasonable view is that, just as the eye, the hand, the foot, and similarly every part of the body each has a definite function, so man may be regarded as having a definite function apart from all these. What, then, can this function be? It is not life; for life is apparently something that man shares with the plants, and it is something peculiar to man that we are looking for. Therefore we must exclude the life of nutrition and growth. There is next what may be called the life of sensation. But this too is apparently shared by man with horses, cattle, and all other animals. There remains what I may call the practical life of the rational part of man's being. But the rational part is twofold: It is rational partly in the sense of being obedient to reason, and partly in the sense of possessing reason and intelligence. The practical life too may be conceived of in two ways,[8] and we must understand by it the life of activity, since this seems to be the more proper meaning of the term.

The function of a human being, then, is an activity of soul in accordance with reason, or not independent of reason. The function of a person of a certain kind, and of such a person who is *good* of his kind—for example, the function of a harpist and the function of a *good* harpist—are in our view generically the same. This view is true of people of all kinds without exception. The superiority in excellence[9] of the good one is simply an addition to the function; for it is a function of a harpist to play the harp, and of a good harpist to play the harp well. If this is so, and if we define the function of a human being as a kind of life, and this life as an activity or action of the soul in conformity with reason; if the function of a good person is such activity or action of a good and noble kind; and if everything is successfully performed when it is performed in accordance with its proper excellence—if all this is so, it follows that the human good is an activity of soul in accordance with virtue or, if there are multiple virtues, in accordance with the best and most complete virtue. But it is necessary to add "in a complete life." For just as one swallow or one day does not make a spring, so one day or a short time does not make someone fortunate or happy. . . .

Chapter 13

Since happiness is an activity of soul in accordance with complete virtue, it is necessary to examine the nature of virtue. For this will perhaps be the best way of studying happiness. . . .

The soul has two parts, one irrational and the other possessing reason. . . . It seems that of the irrational part of the soul, one part is shared by all living things—namely, the vegetative part. I mean the part of the soul that causes nutrition and growth. We may assume that this faculty of the soul exists in all things that receive nutrition, even in embryos; and that it exists in things that are fully grown, since it is more reasonable to suppose that it is the same faculty than that is a different one. It is clear then that the virtue or excellence of this faculty is not distinctively human but is shared by man with all living things. . . .

There seems to be another natural principle of the soul that is irrational and yet in a sense shares in reason. For in a continent or incontinent person we praise the reason and that part of the soul that possesses reason, since it exhorts men rightly and exhorts them to the best conduct. But it is clear that there is in them another principle that is naturally different from reason and fights and contends against reason. For just as the paralyzed parts of the body, when we intend to move them to the right, are drawn away in a contrary direction to the left, so it is with the soul: The impulses of incontinent people run contrary to reason. But there is this difference, however, that while in the body we see that part that is drawn astray, in the soul we do not see it. But it is probably right to suppose with equal certainty that there is in the soul too something different from reason that opposes and thwarts it, although the sense in which it is distinct from reason is immaterial. But it appears that this part too shares in reason, as we said. In a continent person it obeys reason, at least; and in a temperate or courageous person it is probably still more obedient, being absolutely harmonious with reason.

It appears then that the irrational part of the soul is itself twofold; for the vegetative faculty does not participate at all in reason, but the faculty of appetite or of desire in general participates in it more or less, insofar as it is submissive and obedient to reason. It is obedient in the sense in which we speak of "paying attention" to a father or to friends, but not in the sense in which we speak of "paying attention" to mathematics. All correction, rebuke, and exhortation show that the irrational part of the soul is in a sense subject to the influence of reason. But if we are to say that this part too possesses reason, then the part that possesses reason will have two divisions, one possessing reason absolutely and in itself, the other listening to it as a child listens to its father.

Virtue or excellence admits of a distinction that depends on this difference. For we speak of some virtues as intellectual and of others as moral. Wisdom, intelligence and prudence are intellectual virtues, while generosity and temperance are moral virtues. For when we describe a person's character, we do not say that he is wise or intelligent but that he is gentle or temperate. Yet we praise a wise man too for his disposition, and praiseworthy dispositions we call virtues.

Book II

Chapter 1

Virtue or excellence, then, is of two kinds, intellectual and moral. Intellectual virtue is both originated and fostered mainly by teaching, and therefore it demands experience and time. Moral virtue, on the other hand, is the outcome of habit, and accordingly its name "moral" *(ēthikē)* is derived by a slight variation from "habit" *(ethos)*. From this fact it is clear that no moral virtue is implanted in us by nature, for law of nature cannot be altered by habituation. Thus a stone naturally tends to fall downward, and it cannot be habituated or trained to rise upward, even if we were to try to train it by throwing it upward ten thousand times. Nor can fire be trained to sink downward, nor anything else that follows one natural law be trained to follow another. Virtues arise in us neither by nature nor contrary to nature. Nature gives us the capacity of receiving them, and that capacity is perfected by habit.

With regard to the various natural powers that belong to us, we first acquire the proper faculties and afterwards display the activities. This is clearly so with the senses. It was not by seeing frequently or hearing frequently that we acquired the senses of seeing or hearing; on the contrary, it was because we possessed the senses that we made use of them, not by making use of them that we obtained them. But the virtues we acquire by first exercising them, as is the case with all the arts, for it is by doing what we ought to do when we have learned the arts that we learn the arts themselves. For example, we become builders by building and harpists by playing the harp. Similarly it is by doing just acts that we become just, by doing temperate acts that we become temperate, by doing courageous acts that we become courageous. The experience of states is a witness to this truth, for legislators make the citizens good by training the habits. This is the object that all legislators have at heart. If a legislator does not succeed in it, he fails to achieve his purpose, and it constitutes the distinction between a good polity and a bad one.

The causes and means by which any virtue is produced and those by which it is destroyed are the same, and it is equally so with any art. For it is by playing the harp that both good and bad harpists are produced; and the case of builders and all other artisans is similar, since it is by building well that they will be good builders and by building badly that they will be bad builders. If it were not so, there would be no need for anybody to teach them; they would all be born good or bad in their various trades. The case of the virtues is the same. It is by acting in transactions that take place between people that we become either just or unjust. It is by acting in the face of danger and by habituating ourselves to fear or courage that we become either cowardly or courageous. It is much the same with our desires and angry passions. Some people become temperate and gentle, and others become licentious and passionate, according to the way they conduct themselves in particular circumstances. In a word, moral dispositions are the results of activities corresponding to the dispositions themselves. It is our duty therefore to give a certain character to the activities, since dispositions depend on the differences of the activities. Accordingly, it is no small matter how children are trained in habits in their early days; it is an important matter—in fact, it is all-important. . . .

Chapter 4

A difficulty may be raised by our statement that people must become just by doing what is just and temperate by doing what is temperate: If they do what is just and temperate, they are already just and temperate, in the same way that people who do what is grammatical and musical are already grammarians and musicians.

But is not the answer that it is different in the case of the arts? For a person may do something that is grammatical either by chance or at the suggestion of somebody else; hence he will not be a grammarian unless he not only does what is grammatical but does it in a grammatical manner, that is, in virtue of the grammatical knowledge that he possesses.

There is another point of difference between the arts and the virtues. The productions of art have their excellence in themselves. It is enough therefore that when they are produced, they are of a certain character. But actions in accordance with virtue are not, for example, justly or temperately performed because they are in themselves just or temperate. It is necessary that the agent at the time of performing them should satisfy certain conditions: First, he should know what he is doing; second, he should deliberately choose to do it and to do it for its own sake; and third, that he should do it as an instance of a settled and immutable disposition. If it is a question whether a person possesses any art, these conditions (except indeed the condition of knowledge) are not taken into account; but if it is a question of possessing the virtues, mere knowledge is of little or no avail, and it is the other conditions, which are the results of frequently performing just and temperate actions, that are not of slight but of absolute importance. Accordingly, deeds are said to be just and temperate when they are of a kind that just or temperate person would do, and a just and temperate person is not merely one who does these deeds but one who does them in the way that just and the temperate people do them. . . .

Chapter 6

It is not enough to state merely that virtue is a disposition; we must also describe the character of that disposition. It must be laid down that every virtue or excellence has the effect of producing a good condition of that of which it is a virtue or excellence, and of enabling it to perform its function well. Thus the excellence of the eye makes the eye good and makes it function well, since it is by the excellence of the eye that we see well. Similarly, the excellence of a horse makes it excellent and makes it good at racing, carrying its rider, and facing the enemy. If this is true for all things, then the virtue or excellence of man is a disposition that makes a man good and enables him to perform his proper function well. We have already explained how this will be the case, but another way of making it clear will be to study the nature or character of this virtue.

In everything, whether it is continuous or divisible, it is possible to take a greater, a smaller, or an equal part, and this can be done either in respect to the thing itself or relatively to us. The equal part is a mean between excess and deficiency. By the mean in respect to the thing itself, I understand that which is equally distant from both extremes; and this is one and the same thing for everyone. By the mean relative to us, I understand that which is neither too much nor too little; but this is not one thing, nor is it the same for everyone. Thus, if 10 is too much and 2 is too little, we take 6 as a mean in respect to the thing itself, since 6 is as much greater than 2 as it is less than 10. This is a mean in arithmetical proportion. But the mean relative to us must not be ascertained in this way. It does not follow that if 10 pounds of food is too much for a man to eat and 2 is too little, a trainer will order him 6 pounds. For this amount may itself be too much or too little for the person who is to take it: It will be too little, for example, for Milo,[10] but too much for a beginner in gymnastics. It will be the same with running and wrestling; the right amount will vary with the individual. This being so, everyone who understands his business avoids both excess and deficiency;

he seeks and chooses the mean—not the absolute mean, but the mean relative to us.

Every science, then, performs its function well if it looks to the mean and refers the works that it produces to that standard. This is why it is usually said of successful works that it is impossible to take anything from them or to add anything to them; excess or deficiency is fatal to excellence but the mean ensures it. Good artists too, as we say, have an eye to the mean in their works. But virtue, like nature itself, is more accurate and better than any art; therefore virtue will aim at the mean. (I speak of moral virtue, since it is moral virtue that is concerned with emotions and actions, and it is these that admit of excess and deficiency and the mean.) Thus it is possible to go too far, or not to go far enough, in respect to fear, courage, desire, anger, pity, and pleasure and pain generally; and the excess and the deficiency are both wrong. But to experience these emotions at the right times and on the right occasions and toward the right persons and for the right causes and in the right manner is the mean and the best—and this is characteristic of virtue. Similarly there may be excess, deficiency, or the mean in regard to actions. But virtue is concerned with emotions and actions, and here excess is an error and deficiency is a fault, whereas the mean is successful and praiseworthy—and both success and praiseworthiness are characteristics of virtue. It appears then that virtue is a mean, insofar at least as it aims at the mean.

There are many different ways of going wrong; for evil is in its nature infinite, to use the Pythagorean[11] image, but good is finite. But there is only one possible way of going right. Accordingly the former is easy and the latter difficult; it is easy to miss the target but difficult to hit it. This again is a reason why excess and deficiency are characteristics of vice and the mean charactcristic of virtue. "Good is simple, but evil is manifold."[12]

Virtue then is a state of deliberate moral purpose consisting in a mean relative to us, the mean being determined by reason, or as a prudent man would determine it. It is a mean, first, as lying between two vices, the vice of excess on the one hand and the vice of deficiency on the other; and second because, whereas the vices either fall short of or go beyond what is proper in the emotions and actions, virtue not only discovers the mean but embraces it. Accordingly, virtue regarded in its essence or theoretical conception is a mean, but regarded from the point of view of the best and the right, it is an extreme.

But not every action or every emotion admits of a mean. There are some whose very name implies wickedness, for example, the emotions of malice, shamelessness, and envy; and the actions of adultery, theft, and murder. All these, and others like them, are censured as being intrinsically wicked, not the excess or deficiency of them. It is never possible then to be right in respect to them; they are always wrong. Right or wrong in such actions as adultery does not depend on our committing them with the right person, at the right time, or in the right manner; on the contrary, it is wrong to do anything of the kind at all. It would be equally wrong to suppose that there can be a mean or an excess or deficiency in unjust, cowardly, or licentious conduct; for if there were, there would be a mean of an excess or of a deficiency, an excess of an excess and a deficiency of a deficiency. But just as in temperance and courage there can be no excess or deficiency because the mean is, in a sense, an extreme; so too in these cases there cannot be a mean or an excess or deficiency. These acts are wrong, no matter how they are done. For it is a general rule that an excess or deficiency does not admit of a mean, and that a mean does not admit of excess or deficiency.

Chapter 7

It is not enough to lay this down as a general rule; we must apply it to particular cases. In reasoning about actions, general statements are less exact than particular statements, although they are broader. For all action refers to particulars, and it is essential that our theories should harmonize with the particular cases to which they apply. We must take particular virtues, then, from the chart.[13]

In regard to feelings of fear and confidence, courage is the mean. On the side of excess, the person whose fearlessness is excessive has no name (as often happens), but he whose confidence is excessive is foolhardy, while he whose fear is excessive and whose confidence is deficient is a coward.

In respect to pleasures and pains—although not of all pleasures and pains, and to a less extent in respect to pains than to pleasures—the mean is temperance and the excess is licentiousness. Since we never find people who deficient in regard to pleasures, such people have received no name, but we may call them insensible.

In respect to the giving and taking of money, the mean is generosity, and the excess and deficiency are prodigality and stinginess. Here the excess and deficiency take opposite forms; for while the prodigal man is excessive in spending and deficient in taking, the stingy man is excessive in taking and deficient in spending.

For the present we are giving only a rough and summary account of the virtues, and that is sufficient for our purpose.

▶ NOTES

1. The chapter divisions in Welldon's translation have been revised to follow the chapter divisions in the Greek edition in the Oxford Classical Text, edited by Ingram Bywater (Oxford, England: Clarendon Press, 1894), which has become standard. [D. C. ABEL, EDITOR]

2. *ends:* goals [D. C. ABEL]

3. To the Greeks, the city-state *(polis)* was the most advanced form of community, and politics was the enterprise of achieving the good of the city-state. [D. C. ABEL]

4. Aristotle here refers primarily to Plato, under whom he studied for twenty years. [D. C. ABEL]

5. Sardanapallus is the Greek name of King Ashurbanipal of Assyria (668–627 B.C.E.), who was famous for his sensual indulgence. [D. C. ABEL]

6. Aristotle discusses the theoretical life in Book X of the *Nicomachean Ethics* (not included in our reading). [D. C. ABEL]

7. *things mentioned before:* namely, pleasure, honor, and virtue [D. C. ABEL]

8. The practical life of reason can be spoken of in a passive sense, as merely possessing the ability to reason, or in an active sense, as actually exercising this ability. [D. C. ABEL]

9. Depending on the context, the translator renders the Greek word *aretē* as "excellence" (as here) or "virtue." At times he uses the double translation "virtue or excellence." As Aristotle explains later (Book II, Chapter 6), *aretē* is the quality that makes a thing be in good condition and enables it to perform its function well. [D. C. ABEL]

10. Milo of Croton was a famous Greek wrestler of the sixth century B.C.E. [D. C. ABEL]

11. Pythagoras (about 580–500 B.C.E.) was a Greek philosopher and mathematician. [D. C. ABEL]

12. A line—perhaps Pythagorean—of unknown authorship [W. E. C. WELLDON, TRANSLATOR]

13. Aristotle evidently refers to a chart that he used when presenting this material to his students. [D. C. ABEL]

Summa Theologiae

Thomas Aquinas

Thomas Aquinas was born in Roccasecca, Italy, in about 1224. After receiving his initial education from the Benedictine monks at Monte Cassino, he studied at the University of Naples, where he encountered members of the Dominican order. Attracted to the Dominicans, he joined the order despite opposition from his family. He was trained in philosophy and theology in Paris and in Cologne, Germany, under the Dominican Albert (later known as Albert the Great). After being ordained a priest, Aquinas pursued advanced studies in theology at the University of Paris, receiving his degree in 1256. He taught for a few years at the University of Paris and was then assigned to teach at various Dominican schools in Italy. He returned to the University of Paris in 1268, but four years later went back to Italy to establish a new Dominican house of study at the University of Naples. He died in 1274 at Fossanova, Italy, while traveling to Lyons to serve as a papal consultant at the Second Council of Lyons.

Aquinas's major works include the *Summa Contra Gentiles* ("Comprehensive Treatise against the Gentiles"), the *Summa Theologiae* ("Comprehensive Treatise on Theology"), *Disputed Questions* (summaries of debates he conducted on various topics as a professor of theology), and detailed commentaries on the principal works of Aristotle.

Our selection is from Aquinas's "Treatise on Law," a section of the *Summa Theologiae*. Aquinas argues that to be moral means to follow the "natural law." By "natural law" he does not mean the laws of nature, such as the law of gravity, but the moral law that follows from the nature of human beings. Natural law is a subset of eternal law—the law by which God governs the entire universe. According to Aquinas, God directs all creatures by instilling in them natural inclinations. But human beings are subject to eternal law in a special way: Unlike other material creatures, they have reason and free will, which enable them to decide whether and how to fulfill their natural tendencies.

The first precept (command) of natural law is that "good is to be done and pursued, and evil is to be avoided." To specify what the good is for human beings, Aquinas distinguishes three levels of human inclination. As a substance (thing), we are inclined to preserve our own existence; as an animal, to procreate and care for our offspring; as a *rational* animal, to know the truth and live harmoniously with others. Consequently, natural law dictates that we should (1) preserve our own lives, (2) have children and take care of them, and (3) seek the truth and live peacefully in society. To be moral is to follow these commands. As Aquinas explains elsewhere, if the commands come into conflict in some situation, we must use the virtue of prudence to decide which one to follow. Aquinas maintains that these precepts are written in the hearts of all human beings, but that strong passions or corrupt habits can obscure a person's awareness of them.

▶ PART 2, FIRST PART, "TREATISE ON LAW"

Question 91: Of the Various Kinds of Law

First Article: Whether There Is an Eternal Law? . . . [A] law is nothing else but a dictate of practical reason[1] emanating from the ruler who governs a perfect community. Now it is evident, granted that the world is ruled by divine providence . . . , that the whole community of the universe is governed by divine reason. Therefore the very idea of the government of things in God, the ruler of the universe, has the nature of a law. And since the divine reason's conception of things is not subject to time but is eternal, according to Proverbs 8:23, therefore it is that this kind of law must be called eternal . . . .

Second Article: Whether There Is in Us a Natural Law? . . . Law, being a rule and measure, can be in a person in two ways: in one way, as in him that rules and measures; in another way, as in that which is ruled and measured, since a thing is ruled and measured, insofar as it partakes of the rule or measure. Therefore, since all things subject to divine providence are ruled and measured by the eternal law. . . , it is evident that all things partake [in some way] of the eternal law, namely, insofar as, from its being imprinted on them, they derive their respective inclinations to their proper acts and ends. Now among all others, the rational creature is subject to divine providence in the most excellent way, insofar as it partakes of a share of providence, by being provident both for itself and for others. Therefore it has a share of the eternal reason, whereby it has a natural inclination to its proper act and end; and this participation of the eternal law in the rational creature is called the natural law. . . .

Question 94: Of the Natural Law

Second Article: Whether the Natural Law Contains Several Precepts, or Only One? . . . A certain order is to be found in those things that are apprehended universally. For that which, before aught else, falls under apprehension is *being*, the notion of which is included in all things whatsoever a man apprehends. Therefore the first indemonstrable principle is that *the same thing cannot be affirmed and denied at the same time*, which is based on the notion of *being* and *not-being*; and on this principle all others are based, as is stated in [Aristotle's] *Metaphysics*, Book IV, Chapter 3. Now as *being* is the first thing that falls under the apprehension simply, so *good* is the first thing that falls under the apprehension of the practical reason, which is directed to action, since every agent acts for an end under the aspect of good. Consequently, the first principle in the practical reason is one founded on the notion of good, namely, that *good is that which all things seek after.*[2] Hence this is the first precept of law, that *good is to be done and pursued, and evil is to be avoided*. All other precepts of the natural law are based upon this, so that whatever the practical reason naturally apprehends as man's good (or evil) belongs to the precepts of the natural law as something to be done or avoided.

Since, however, good has the nature of an end, and evil, the nature of a contrary, hence it is that all those things to which man has a natural inclination, are naturally apprehended by reason as being good, and consequently as objects of pursuit, and their contraries as evil, and objects of avoidance. Therefore, according to the order of natural inclinations, is the order of the precepts of the natural law. [First, there is in man] an inclination to good in accordance with the nature which he has in common with all substances; inasmuch as every substance seeks the preservation of its own being, according to its nature; and by reason of this inclination, whatever is a means of preserving human life and warding off its obstacles, belongs to the natural law. Secondly, there is in man an inclination to things that pertain to him more specially, according to that nature which he has in common with other animals; and in virtue of this inclination, those things are said to belong to the natural law, *which nature has taught to all animals,*[3] such as sexual intercourse, education of offspring and so forth. Thirdly, there is in man an inclination to good, according to the nature of his reason, which nature is proper to him; thus man has a natural inclination to know the truth about God, and to live in society; and in this respect, whatever pertains to this inclination belongs to the natural law—for instance, to shun ignorance, to avoid offending those among whom one has to live, and other such things regarding the above inclination. . . .

Fourth Article: Whether the Natural Law Is the Same in All Men? . . . To the natural law belong those things to which a man is inclined naturally, and among these it is proper to man to be inclined to act according to reason. Now the process of reason is from the common to the proper, as stated in [Aristotle's] *Physics,* Book I, Chapter 1. The speculative reason, however, is differently situated in this matter, from the practical reason. For, since the speculative reason [deals] chiefly with necessary things, which cannot be otherwise than they are, its proper conclusions, like the universal principles, contain the truth without fail. The practical reason, on the other hand, [deals] with contingent matters, about which human actions are concerned; and consequently, although there is necessity in the general principles, the more we descend to matters of detail, the more frequently we encounter defects. Accordingly, then, in speculative matters truth is the same in all men, both as to principles and as to conclusions, although the truth is not known to all as regards the conclusions, but only as regards the principles, which are called *common notions.*[4] But in matters of action, truth or practical rectitude is not the same for all as to matters of detail, but only as to the general principles; and where there is the same rectitude in matters of detail, it is not equally known to all.

It is therefore evident that, as regards the general principles whether of speculative or of practical reason, truth or rectitude is the same for all and is equally known by all. As to the proper conclusions of the speculative reason, the truth is the same for all, but is not equally known to all; thus it is true for all that the three angles of a triangle are together equal to two right angles, although it is not known to all. But as to the proper conclusions of the practical reason, neither is the truth or rectitude the same for all, nor, where it is the same, is it equally known by all. Thus it is right and true for all to act according to reason; and from this principle it follows as a proper conclusion, that goods entrusted to another should be restored to their owner. Now this is true for the majority of cases, but it may happen in a particular case that it would be injurious, and therefore unreasonable, to restore goods held in trust; for instance, if they are claimed for the purpose of fighting against one's country. And this principle will be found to fail the more, according as we descend further into detail, e.g., if one were to say that goods held in trust should be restored with such and such a guarantee, or in such and such a way; because the greater the number of conditions added, the greater the number of ways in which the principle may fail, so that it be not right to restore or not to restore.

Consequently we must say that the natural law, as to general principles, is the same for all, both as to rectitude and as to knowledge. But as to certain matters of detail, which are conclusions, as it were, of those general principles, it is the same for all in the majority of cases, both as to rectitude and as to knowledge; and yet in some few cases it may fail, both as to rectitude, by reason of certain obstacles (just as natures subject to generation and corruption fail in some few cases on account of some obstacle), and as to knowledge, since in some the reason is perverted by passion, or evil habit, or an evil disposition of nature. Thus formerly, theft, although it is expressly contrary to the natural law, was not considered wrong among the Germans, as Julius Caesar relates.[5] . . .

Fifth Article: Whether the Natural Law Can Be Changed? . . . A change in the natural law may be understood in two ways. First, by way of addition. In this sense nothing hinders the natural law from being changed, since many things for the benefit of human life have been added over and above the natural law, both by the divine law and by human laws.

Secondly, a change in the natural law may be understood by way of subtraction, so that what previously was according to the natural law, ceases to be so. In this sense, the natural law is altogether unchangeable in its first principles. But in its secondary principles, which, as we have said (Fourth Article), are certain detailed proximate conclusions drawn from the first principles, the natural law is not changed so that what it prescribes be not right in most cases. But it may be changed in some particular cases of rare occurrence, through some special causes hindering the observance of such precepts, as stated above. . . .

Sixth Article: Whether the Natural Law Can Be Abolished from the Heart of Man? . . . As stated above (Fourth and Fifth Articles), there belong to the natural law, first, certain most general precepts, which are known to all; and secondly, certain secondary and more detailed precepts, which are, as it were, conclusions following closely from first principles. As to those general principles, the natural law, in the abstract, can no wise be blotted out from men's hearts. But it is blotted out in the case of a particular action, insofar as reason is hindered from applying the general principle to a particular point of practice, on account of concupiscence[6] or some other passion. . . . But as to the other, i.e., the secondary precepts, the natural law can be blotted out from the human heart, either by evil persuasions, just as in speculative matters errors occur in respect of necessary conclusions; or by vicious customs and corrupt habits, as among some men, theft, and even unnatural vices, as the Apostle [Paul] states (Romans 1:24), were not esteemed sinful.

▶ NOTES

1. *practical reason:* reason as used to direct practical activity. Practical reason is contrasted with *speculative reason,* which is reason as directed toward knowing the truth for its own sake. As Aquinas explains, the first thing practical reason apprehends is the *good* (the goal of every practical action), whereas the first thing speculative reason apprehends is *being* (the goal of our desire to know reality). [D.C.A., ed.]

2. Aristotle, *Nicomachean Ethics,* Book I, Chapter 1 [D.C.A.]

3. *Digest,* Book I, Title 1, no. 1. The *Digest* is a codification of the works of classical jurists published by the Roman emperor Justinian in 533. The quotation cited here is attributed to the Roman jurist Ulpian (died 228 C.E.). [D.C.A.]

4. *common notions:* notions (*conceptiones,* "conceptions") common to all human beings. The term comes from Boethius, *How Substances Can Be Good in Virtue of Their Existence without Being Absolute Goods,* point 1. Boethius (about 480–524) was a Roman statesperson, philosopher, and theologian. [D.C.A.]

5. in *The Gallic War,* Book VI, Chapter 23 [D.C.A.]

6. *concupiscence:* the human tendency to let the desire for sensual pleasure overpower reason [D.C.A.]

Summa Theologiae

Thomas Aquinas

Thomas Aquinas was born in Roccasecca, Italy, in about 1224. After receiving his initial education from the Benedictine monks at Monte Cassino, he studied at the University of Naples, where he encountered members of the Dominican order. Attracted to the Dominicans, he joined the order despite opposition from his family. He was trained in philosophy and theology in Paris and Cologne, Germany, under the Dominican Albert (later known as Albert the Great). After being ordained a priest, Aquinas pursued advanced studies in theology at the University of Paris, receiving his degree in 1256. He taught for a few years at the University of Paris and was then assigned to teach at various Dominican schools in Italy. Aquinas returned to the University of Paris in 1268, but four years later he went back to Italy to establish a new Dominican house of study at the University of Naples. He died in 1274 at Fossanova, Italy, while traveling to Lyons to serve as a papal consultant at the Second Council of Lyons.

Aquinas's major works include the *Summa Contra Gentiles* ("Comprehensive Treatise against the Gentiles"), the *Summa Theologiae* ("Comprehensive Treatise on Theology"), *Disputed Questions* (summaries of debates he conducted on various topics as a professor of theology), and detailed commentaries on the principal works of Aristotle.

Our reading is taken from three "articles" (subdivisions) of the "question" (a larger division) in the *Summa Theologiae* entitled "Of Lying." In the first article, "Whether Lying Is Opposed to Truth?" Aquinas maintains that a lie can be defined in terms of three factors (the principal one being the intention to deceive) and that all three are opposed to truth. Since truth is a virtue, he explains, lying is a vice. The second article asks "Whether Lies Are Sufficiently Divided into Officious, Jocose, and Mischievous Lies?" Aquinas explains and accepts this traditional classification of lies, but also finds a basis for defending another, more elaborate traditional classification schema (one with eight categories). In the final article, "Whether Every Lie is a Sin?," Aquinas argues that all lies are sinful. We may not even lie to protect others from injury, though we may protect others by prudently holding back the truth.

▼

▶ PART 2, SECOND PART

Question 110: Of Lying

First Article: Whether Lying Is Always Opposed to Truth? . . . The virtue of truth—and consequently the opposite vices—regards a manifestation made by certain signs, and this manifestation or statement is an act of reason comparing sign with the thing signified; because every representation consists in comparison, which is the proper[1] act of the reason. [Hence,] though dumb animals manifest something, yet they do not intend to manifest any-

---

Thomas Aquinas, *Summa Theologiae* (selection 3, "Of Lying"). From *The "Summa Theologica" of St. Thomas Aquinas,* Part II, Second Part, QQ. CI–CXL, trans. Fathers of the English Dominican Province (New York: Benziger Brothers, 1922). (Not copyrighted)

thing; but they do something by natural instinct, and a manifestation is the result. But when this manifestation or statement is a moral act, it must needs be voluntary, and dependent on the intention of the will. Now the proper object of a manifestation or statement is the true or the false. And the intention of a bad will may bear on two things: one of which is that a falsehood may be told, while the other is the proper effect of a false statement—namely, that someone may be deceived.

Accordingly, if these three things concur—namely, falsehood of what is said, the will to tell a falsehood, and finally the intention to deceive—then there is falsehood: *materially,* since what is said is false; *formally,* on account of the will to tell an untruth; and *effectively,* on account of the will to impart a falsehood.[2]

However, the essential notion of a lie is taken from formal falsehood, from the fact, namely, that a person intends to say what is false; [thus] the word *mendacium* (lie) is derived from its being in opposition to the mind *(mens).* Consequently if one says what is false, thinking it to be true, it is false materially, but not formally, because the falseness is beside the intention of the speaker—so that it is not a perfect lie, since what is beside the speaker's intention is accidental for which reason it cannot be a specific difference.[3] If, on the other hand, one utters a falsehood formally, through having the will to deceive, even if what one says be true, yet inasmuch as this is a voluntary and moral act, it contains falseness essentially and truth accidentally, and attains the specific nature of a lie. . . .

Second Article: Whether Lies Are Sufficiently Divided into Officious, Jocose, and Mischievous Lies?[4] . . . Lies may be divided in three ways. First, with respect to their nature as lies: and this is the proper and essential division of lying. In this way, according to the Philosopher[5] (*Nicomachean Ethics,* Book IV, Chapter 7), lies are of two kinds, namely: the lie which goes beyond the truth, and this belongs to *boasting;* and the lie which stops short of the truth, and this belongs to *irony.* This division is an essential division of lying itself, because lying as such is opposed to truth, as stated in the preceding Article: and truth is a kind of equality, to which more and less are in essential opposition.

Secondly, lies may be divided with respect to their nature as sins, and with regard to those things that aggravate or diminish the sin of lying, on the part of the end intended. Now the sin of lying is aggravated, if by lying a person intends to injure another, and this is called a *mischievous* lie; while the sin of lying is diminished if it be directed to some good—either of pleasure (and then it is a *jocose* lie), or of usefulness (and then we have the *officious* lie, whereby it is intended to help another person, or to save him from being injured). In this way lies are divided into the three kinds [mentioned].

Thirdly, lies are divided in a more general way, with respect to their relation to some end, whether or not this increases or diminishes their gravity: and in this way the division comprises eight kinds [namely, lies that (1) concern religious doctrine, (2) profit no one and injure someone, (3) profit someone and injure someone else, (4) are told simply from a desire to deceive, (5) are told from a desire to please, (6) injure no one and save someone money, (7) injure no one and save someone from death, (8) injure no one and save someone from defilement of the body].[6] Here the first three kinds are contained under *mischievous lies,* which are either against God (and then we have the lie *in religious doctrine*), or against man, and this either with the sole intention of injuring him (and then it is the second kind of lie, which *profits no one and injures someone*) or with the intention of injuring one and at the same time profiting another (and this is the third kind of lie, *which profits one and injures another*). Of these, the first is the most grievous, because sins against God are always more grievous. . . . And the second is more grievous than the third, since the latter's gravity is diminished by the intention of profiting another.

After these three, which aggravate the sin of lying, we have a fourth, which has its own measure of gravity without addition or diminution, and this is the lie which is told *out of mere lust of lying and deceiving.* This proceeds from the habit, wherefore the Philosopher says (*Nicomachean Ethics,* Book IV, Chapter 7) that *the liar, since he lies from habit, delights in lying.*

The four kinds that follow lessen the gravity of the sin of lying. For the fifth kind is the jocose lie, which is told *with a desire to please:* and the remaining three are comprised under the officious lie, wherein something useful to another person is intended. This usefulness regards either external things, and then we have the sixth kind of lie, which *profits someone in saving his money;* or his body, and this is the seventh kind, which *saves a man from death;* or the morality of his virtue, and this is the eighth kind, which *saves him from unlawful defilement of his body.*

Now it is evident that the greater the good intended, the more is the sin of lying diminished in gravity. [Hence] a careful consideration of the matter will show that these various kinds of lies are enumerated in their order of gravity: since the useful good is better than the pleasurable good, and life of the body than money, and virtue than the life of the body. . . .

Third Article: Whether Every Lie Is a Sin? . . . An action that is naturally evil in respect of its genus can by no means be good and lawful, since in order for an action to be good it must be right in every respect: because good results from a complete cause, while evil results from any single defect, as Dionysius[7] asserts (*On the Divine Names,* Chapter 4). Now a lie is evil in respect of its genus, since it is an action bearing on undue matter. For as words are naturally signs of intellectual acts, it is unnatural and undue for anyone to signify by words something that is not in his mind. Hence the Philosopher says (*Nicomachean Ethics,* Book IV, Chapter 7) that *lying is in itself evil and to be shunned, while truthfulness is good and worthy of praise.* Therefore every lie is a sin, as also Augustine declares (*Against Lying,* Chapter 21). . . .

A lie is sinful not only because it injures one's neighbour, but also on account of its inordinateness. . . . Now it is not allowed to make use of anything inordinate in order to ward off injury or defects from another: as neither is it lawful to steal in order to give an alms, except perhaps in a case of necessity when all things are common. Therefore it is not lawful to tell a lie in order to deliver another from any danger whatever. Nevertheless it is lawful to hide the truth prudently, by keeping it back, as Augustine says (*Against Lying,* Chapter 10).

▶ NOTES

1. *proper:* distinctive, belonging characteristically or peculiarly to [D.C.A., ed.]

2. The *matter* of a lie its content; the *form* of a lie is that which makes the content a lie; the *effect* of a lie is that someone is deceived. [D.C.A.]

3. An attribute is *accidental* to something if it is not part of the thing's essence. Since a thing's essence includes the attributes that make it a particular *species* (subcategory) of a *genus* (a larger category), an accidental attribute cannot be a *specific difference* (something that differentiates it from other species in the genus). [D.C.A.]

4. This threefold division of lies derives from a traditional exposition of Psalms 5:6, "Thou destroyest those who speak lies" (Revised Standard Version). [D.C.A.]

5. *the Philosopher:* Aristotle (384–322 B.C.E.) [D.C.A.]

6. The list comes from Augustine, *Against Lying,* Chapter 14. Augustine (354–430) was a north African Christian theologian. [D.C.A.]

7. Dionysius was the name given to the author of certain Christian theological works in the early sixth century, mistakenly identified with Dionysius the Areopagite, who is mentioned in the Acts of Apostles (17:24). He is now called Pseudo-Dionysius. [D.C.A.]

Fifteen Sermons Preached at the Rolls Chapel

Joseph Butler

Joseph Butler was born in Wantage, England, in 1692. He studied at Oriel College of Oxford University and received his bachelor's degree in 1718. That same year he was ordained a priest in the Church of England. In 1719 Butler was appointed preacher at the Rolls Chapel in London, a post he held until 1726. He became rector of Stanhope in 1725 and for several years served as parish priest in various parishes. In 1736 Butler was named chaplain to Queen Caroline, the wife of King George II. After Queen Caroline's death in 1737, he became Bishop of Bristol. He returned to the royal household as chaplain to King George II in 1746. In 1750 Butler was appointed Bishop of Durham. He died in 1752 in Bath, England. His major publications are *Fifteen Sermons Preached at the Rolls Chapel* (1726) and *The Analogy of Religion, Natural and Revealed, to the Constitution and Course of Nature* (1736).

Our reading is from the eleventh of Butler's *Fifteen Sermons,* "Upon the Love of Our Neighbor." Butler's aim is to refute the view that self-love is incompatible with love of neighbor. He explains that our human nature contains not only a general desire for happiness (an internal state), but also a desire for external objects. External objects satisfy our affections, passions, and appetites, and it is by obtaining these objects that we fulfill our general desire for happiness. While self-love seeks external objects simply as a means to happiness, another part of our nature seeks these objects as such.

Just as there is no inherent conflict between self-love and a desire for food or honor, so there is no inherent conflict between self-love and a desire to promote the welfare of our neighbor. Self-love is no more incompatible with love of neighbor than with love of reputation or music. "There is no peculiar contrariety between self-love and benevolence; no greater competition between these, than between any other particular affections and self-love." A life devoted to benevolence has certain advantages over one that focuses on some other passion, such as ambition. For example, while both the benevolent person and the ambitious person find pleasure if they succeed in their efforts, if they fail, the benevolent person takes satisfaction in the very effort to benefit others—especially if he or she believes that benevolent actions meet with the approval of an infinite Being. In short, "benevolence and the pursuit of particular passions, and public good has at least as great respect to self-love and the pursuit of private good, as any other particular passions and their respective pursuits."

Reprinted from Joseph Butler, *The Fifteen Sermons Preached at the Rolls Chapel.* In *The Works of Joseph Butler,* ed. W. E. Gladstone. Vol. 2. Oxford, England: Clarendon Press, 1896 (updated stylistically).

Sermon XI. Upon the Love of Our Neighbor

And if there be any other commandment, it is briefly comprehended in this saying, namely, Thou shalt love thy neighbor as thyself.

—*Romans 13:9*

. . . Every man has a general desire of his own happiness; and likewise a variety of particular affections, passions, and appetites to particular external objects. The former proceeds from, or is, self-love and seems inseparable from all sensible[1] creatures, who can reflect upon themselves and their own interest or happiness, so as to have that interest an object to their minds. What is to be said of the latter is that they proceed from, or together make up, that particular nature according to which man is made. The object the former pursues is somewhat[2] internal, our own happiness, enjoyment, satisfaction—whether we have, or have not, a distinct particular perception what it is, or wherein it consists. The objects of the latter are this or that particular external thing, which the affections tend towards, and of which it has always a particular idea or perception. The principle we call self-love never seeks anything external for the sake of the thing, but only as a means of happiness or good: Particular affections rest in the external things themselves. One belongs to man as a reasonable creature reflecting upon his own interest or happiness. The other [affections], though quite distinct from reason, are as much a part of human nature.

That all particular appetites and passions are towards *external things themselves,* distinct from the *pleasure arising from them,* is manifested from hence—that there could not be this pleasure, were it not for that prior suitableness between the object and the passion. There could be no enjoyment or delight from one thing more than another, from eating food more than from swallowing a stone, if there were not an affection or appetite to one thing more than another.

Every particular affection, even the love of our neighbor, is as really our own affection, as self-love; and the pleasure arising from its gratification is as much my own pleasure, as the pleasure self-love would have, from knowing I myself should be happy some time hence, would be my own pleasure. And if, because every particular affection is a man's own, and the pleasure arising from its gratification his own pleasure, or pleasure to himself, such particular affection must be called self-love. According to this way of speaking, no creature whatever can possibly act but merely from self-love; and every action and every affection whatever is to be resolved up into this one principle. But then this is not the language of mankind; or, if it were, we should want words to express the difference between the principle of an action proceeding from cool consideration that it will be to my own advantage, and an action (suppose of revenge, or of friendship) by which a man runs upon certain ruin, to do evil or good to another. It is manifest [that] the principles of these actions are totally different, and so want different words to be distinguished by. All that they agree in is that they both proceed from, and are done to gratify, an inclination in a man's self. But the principle or inclination in one case is self-love; in the other, hatred or love of another. There is then a distinction between the cool principle of self-love, or general desire of our own happiness, as one part of our nature and one principle of action; and the particular affections towards particular external objects, as another part of our nature and another principle of action. How much soever therefore is to be allowed for self-love, yet it cannot be allowed to be the whole of our inward constitution because, you see, there are other parts or principles which come into it.

Further, private happiness or good is all which self-love can make us desire, or be concerned about. In having this consists its gratification: It is an affection to ourselves—a regard to our own interest, happiness, and private good. And in the proportion a man has this, he is interested, or a lover of himself. Let this be kept in mind, because there is commonly—as I shall presently have occasion to observe—another sense put upon these words. On the other hand, particular affections tend towards particular external things: These are their objects; having these is their end.[3] In this consists their gratification, no matter whether it be, or be not, upon the whole, our interest or happiness. An action done from the former of these principles is called an interested action. An action proceeding from any of the latter has its denomination of passionate, ambitious, friendly, revengeful, or any other, from the particular appetite or affection from which it proceeds. Thus self-love as one part of human nature, and the several particular principles as the other part, are themselves their objects and ends, stated and shown.

From hence it will be easy to see how far, and in what ways, each of these can contribute and be subservient to the private good of the individual. Happiness does not consist in self-love. The desire of happiness is no more the thing itself, than the desire of riches is the possession or enjoyment of them. People may love themselves with the most entire and unbounded affection, and yet be extremely miserable. Neither can self-love any way help them out, but by setting them on work to get rid of the causes of their misery, to gain or make use of those objects which are by nature adapted to afford satisfaction. Happiness or satisfaction consists only in the enjoyment of those objects which are by nature suited to our several particular appetites, passions, and affections. So that if self-love wholly engrosses us and leaves no room for any other principle, there can be absolutely no such thing at all as happiness or enjoyment of any kind whatever, since happiness consists in the gratification of particular passions, which supposes the having of them. Self-love then does not constitute *this* or *that* to be our interest or good; but, our interest or good being constituted by nature and supposed, self-love only puts us upon obtaining and securing it.

Therefore, if it be possible that self-love may prevail and exert itself in a degree or manner which is not subservient to this end, then it will not follow, that our interest will be promoted in proportion to the degree in which that principle engrosses us and prevails over others. Nay further, the private and contracted affection, when it is not subservient to this end (private good) may, for any thing that appears, have a direct contrary tendency and effect. And if we will consider the matter, we shall see that it often really has. *Disengagement* is absolutely necessary to enjoyment. And a person may have so steady and fixed an eye upon his own interest, whatever he places it in, as may hinder him from *attending* to many gratifications within his reach, which others have their minds free and open to. Overfondness for a child is not generally thought to be for its advantage. And if there be any guess to be made from appearances, surely that character we call selfish is not the most promising for happiness. Such a temper may plainly be, and exert itself in a degree and manner which may give unnecessary and useless solicitude and anxiety, in a degree and manner which may prevent obtaining the means and materials of enjoyment, as well as the making use of them. Immoderate self-love does very ill consult its own interest; and, how much soever a paradox it may appear, it is certainly true that even from self-love we should endeavor to get over all inordinate regard to and consideration of ourselves. Every one of our passions and affections has its natural stint and bound, which may easily be exceeded; whereas our enjoyments can possibly be but in a determinate measure and degree. Therefore such excess of the affection, since it cannot procure any enjoyment, must in all cases be useless, but is generally attended with inconveniences and often is downright pain and misery. This holds as much with regard to self-love as to all other affections. The natural degree of it, so far as it sets us on work to gain and make use of the materials of satisfaction, may be to our real advantage. But beyond or besides this, it is in several respects an inconvenience and disadvantage. Thus it appears that private interest is so far from being likely to be promoted in proportion to the degree in which self-love engrosses us and prevails over all other principles; that the contracted affection may be so prevalent as to disappoint itself and even contradict its own end, private good.

[Someone may argue:] "But who, except the most sordidly covetous, ever thought there was any rivalship between the love of greatness, honor, power, or between sensual appetites, and self-love? No, there is a perfect harmony between them. It is by means of these particular appetites and affections that self-love is gratified in enjoyment, happiness, and satisfaction. The competition and rivalship is between self-love and the love of our neighbor—that affection which leads us out of ourselves, makes us regardless of our own interest, and substitute that of another in its stead." Whether then there be any peculiar competition and contrariety in this case, shall now be considered.

Self-love and interestedness was stated to consist in or be an affection to ourselves, a regard to our own private good. It is therefore distinct from benevolence, which is an affection to the good of our fellow creatures. But that benevolence is distinct from (that is, not the same thing with) self-love, is no reason for its being looked upon with any peculiar suspicion, because every principle whatever, by means of which self-love is gratified, is distinct from it. And all things which are distinct from each other are equally so. A man has an affection or aversion to another; that one of these tends to and is gratified by doing good, that the other tends to and is gratified by doing harm, does not in the least alter the respect which either one or the other of these inward feelings has to self-love. We use the word *property* so as to exclude any other persons having an interest in that of which we say a particular man has the property. And we often use the word *selfish* so as to exclude in the same manner all regards to the good of others. But the cases are not parallel: For though that exclusion is really part of the idea of property; yet such positive exclusion, or bringing this peculiar disregard to the good of others into the idea of self-love, is in reality adding to the idea, or changing it from what it was before stated to consist in, namely, in an affection to ourselves. This being the whole idea of self-love, it can no otherwise exclude goodwill or love of others, than merely by not including it—no otherwise than it excludes love of arts or reputation, or of anything else. Neither on the other hand does benevolence, any more than love of arts or of reputation, exclude self-love. Love of our neighbor then has just the same respect to, is no more distant from, self-love, than hatred of our neighbor, or than love or hatred of anything else.

Thus the principles from which men rush upon certain ruin for the destruction of an enemy, and for the preservation of a friend, have the same respect to the private affection, and are equally interested or equally disinterested; and it is of no avail, whether they are said to be one or the other. Therefore to those who are shocked to hear virtue spoken of as disinterested, it may be allowed that it is indeed absurd to speak thus of it; unless hatred, several particular instances of vice, and all the common affections and aversions in mankind are acknowledged to be disinterested too. Is there any less inconsistence between the love of inanimate things, or of creatures merely sensitive,[4] and self-love; than between self-love and the love of our neighbor? Is desire of and delight in the happiness of another any more a diminution of self-love, than desire of and delight in the esteem of another? They are both equally desire of and delight in somewhat external to ourselves: Either both or neither are so. The object of self-love is expressed in the term *self;* and every appetite of sense and every particular affection of the heart are equally interested or disinterested, because the objects of them all are equally self or somewhat else. Whatever ridicule therefore the mention of a disinterested principle or action may be supposed to lie open to, must, upon the matter being thus stated, relate to ambition; and every appetite and particular affection, as much as to benevolence. And indeed all the ridicule and all the grave perplexity of which this subject has had its full share, is merely from words. The most intelligible way of speaking of it seems to be this: that self-love and the actions done in consequence of it (for these will presently appear to be the same as to this question) are interested; that particular affections towards external objects and the actions done in consequence of those affections are not so. But everyone is at liberty to use words as he pleases. All that is here insisted upon is that ambition, revenge, benevolence, all particular passions whatever, and the actions they produce, are equally interested or disinterested.

Thus it appears that there is no peculiar contrariety between self-love and benevolence; no greater competition between these, than between any other particular affections and self-love. This relates to the affections themselves. Let us now see whether there be any peculiar contrariety between the respective courses of life which these affections lead to; whether there be any greater competition between the pursuit of private and of public good, than between any other particular pursuits and that of private good.

There seems no other reason to suspect that there is any such peculiar contrariety, but only that the course of action which benevolence leads to, has a more direct tendency to promote the good of others, than that course of action which love of reputation, suppose, or any other particular affection leads to. But that any affection tends to the happiness of another, does not hinder its tending to one's own happiness too. That others enjoy the benefit of the air and the light of the sun, does not hinder but that these are as much one's own private advantage now, as they would be if we had the property of them exclusive of all others. So a pursuit which tends to promote the good of another, yet may have as great [a] tendency to promote private interest as a pursuit which does not tend to the good of another at all, or which is mischievous to him. All particular affections whatever—resentment, benevolence, love of arts—equally lead to a course of action for their own gratification, that is, the gratification of ourselves; and the gratification of each gives delight. So far, then, it is manifest they have all the same respect to private interest. Now take into consideration further, concerning these three pursuits, that the end of the first is the harm, of the second, the good of another, of the last, somewhat indifferent. And is there any necessity that these additional considerations should alter the respect which we before saw these three pursuits had to private interest; or render any one of them less conducive to it, than any other? Thus one man's affection is to honor as his end, in order to obtain which he thinks no pains too great. Suppose another with such a singularity of mind as to have the same affection to public good as his end, which he endeavors with the same labor to obtain. In case of success, surely the man of benevolence has as great enjoyment as the man of ambition—they both equally having the end their affections, in the same degree, tended to. But in case of disappointment, the benevolent man has clearly the advantage; since endeavoring to do good, considered as a virtuous pursuit, is gratified by its own consciousness—that is, is in a degree its own reward.

And as to these two, or benevolence and any other particular passions whatever, considered in a further view, as forming a general temper, which more or less disposes us for enjoyment of all the common blessings of life, distinct from their own gratification—is benevolence less the temper of tranquility and freedom than ambition or covetousness? Does the benevolent man appear less easy with himself, from his love to his neighbor? Does he less relish his being? Is there any peculiar gloom seated on his face? Is his mind less open to entertainment, to any particular gratification? Nothing is more manifest than that being in good humor, which is benevolence whilst it lasts, is itself the temper of satisfaction and enjoyment.

Suppose then a man sitting down to consider how he might become most easy to himself and attain the greatest pleasure he could—all that which is his real natural happiness. This can only consist in the enjoyment of those objects which are by nature adapted to our several faculties. These particular enjoyments make up the sum total of our happiness, and they are supposed to arise from riches, honors, and the gratification of sensual appetites. Be it so; yet none profess themselves so completely happy in these enjoyments, but that there is room left in the mind for others, if they were presented to them. Nay, these, as much as they engage us, are not thought so high, but that human nature is capable even of greater.

Now there have been persons in all ages who have professed that they found satisfaction in the exercise of charity, in the love of their neighbor, in endeavoring to promote the happiness of all they had to do with, and in the pursuit of what is just, and right, and good, as the general bent of their mind, and end of their life; and that doing an action of baseness or cruelty would be as great violence to *their* self, as much breaking in upon their nature as any external force. Persons of this character would add, if they might be heard, that they consider themselves as acting in the view of an infinite Being, who is in a much higher sense the object of reverence and of love than all the world besides, and therefore they could have no more enjoyment from a wicked action done under his eye, than the persons to whom they are making their apology could, if all mankind were the spectators of it; and that the satisfaction of approving themselves to his unerring judgment, to whom they thus refer all their actions, is a more continued settled satisfaction than any this world can afford; as also that they have, no less than others, a mind free and open to all the common innocent gratifications of it, such as they are. And if we go no further, does there appear any absurdity in this? Will anyone take upon him to say that a man cannot find his account in this general course of life, as much as in the most unbounded ambition and the excesses of pleasure? Or that such a person has not consulted so well for himself, for the satisfaction and peace of his own mind, as the ambitious or dissolute man?

And though the consideration that God himself will in the end justify their taste and support their cause, is not formally to be insisted upon here; yet thus much comes in, that all enjoyments whatever are much more clear and unmixed from the assurance that they will end well. Is it certain then that there is nothing in these pretensions to happiness, especially when there are not wanting persons who have supported themselves with satisfactions of this kind in sickness, poverty, disgrace, and in the very pangs of death, whereas it is manifest all other enjoyments fail in these circumstances? This surely looks suspicious[5] of having somewhat in it. Self-love methinks[6] should be alarmed. May she not possibly pass over greater pleasures than those she is so wholly taken up with?

The short of the matter is no more than this: Happiness consists in the gratification of certain affections, appetites, passions, with objects which are by nature adapted to them. Self-love may indeed set us on work to gratify these; but happiness or enjoyment has no immediate connection with self-love, but arises from such gratification alone. Love of our neighbor is one of those affections. This, considered as a virtuous principle, is gratified by a consciousness of *endeavoring* to promote the good of others; but considered as a natural affection, its gratification consists in the actual *accomplishment* of this endeavor. Now indulgence or gratification of this affection, whether in that consciousness, or this accomplishment, has the same respect to interest as indulgence of any other affection: They equally proceed from or do not proceed from self-love; they equally include or equally exclude this principle. Thus it appears, that *benevolence and the pursuit of public good has at least as great respect to self-love and the pursuit of private good, as any other particular passions and their respective pursuits. . . .*

The general mistake that there is some greater inconsistence between endeavoring to promote the good of another and self-interest, than between self-interest and pursuing anything else, seems, as has already been hinted, to arise from our notions of property, and to be carried on by this property's being supposed to be itself our happiness or good . People are so very much taken up with this one subject that they seem from it to have formed a general way of thinking, which they apply to other things that they have nothing to do with. . . .

For, if property and happiness are one and the same thing, as by increasing the property of another, you lessen your own property, so by promoting the happiness of another, you must lessen your own happiness. But whatever occasioned the mistake, I hope it has been fully proved to be one, as it has been proved that there is no peculiar rivalship or competition between self-love and benevolence: that as there may be a competition between these two, so there may also between any particular affection whatever and self-love; that every particular affection, benevolence among the rest, is subservient to self-love by being the instrument of private enjoyment; and that in one respect benevolence contributes more to private interest (that is, enjoyment or satisfaction) than any other of the particular common affections, as it is in a degree its own gratification.

And to all these things may be added that religion, from whence arises our strongest obligation to benevolence, is so far from disowning the principle of self-love, that it often addresses itself to that very principle, and always to the mind in that state when reason presides. And there can no access be had to the understanding, but by convincing men that the course of life we would persuade them to is not contrary to their interest. It may be allowed, without any prejudice to the cause of virtue and religion, that our ideas of happiness and misery are of all our ideas the nearest and most important to us; that they will—nay, if you please, that they ought to—prevail over those of order, and beauty, and harmony, and proportion, if there should ever be, as it is impossible there ever should be, any inconsistence between them (though these last too, as expressing the fitness of actions, are real as truth itself). Let it be allowed, though virtue or moral rectitude does indeed consist in affection to and pursuit of what is right and good, as such, yet, that when we sit down in a cool hour, we can neither justify to ourselves this or any other pursuit till we are convinced that it will be for our happiness, or at least not contrary to it.

▶ NOTES

1. *sensible:* capable of sensation [D. C. Abel, editor]
2. *somewhat:* something [D. C. Abel]
3. *end:* goal [D. C. Abel]
4. *sensitive:* capable of sensation [D. C. Abel]
5. *suspicious:* suspected; expected [D. C. Abel]
6. *methinks:* it seems to me [D. C. Abel]

What Do Women Want in a Moral Theory?

Annette C. Baier

Annette C. Baier was born in 1929 in Queenstown, New Zealand. She attended Otago University in New Zealand, where she received her bachelor's degree in 1951 and her master's degree the following year. She then attended Oxford University, receiving a bachelor of philosophy degree in 1954. Baier taught at the University of Aberdeen in Scotland for a year and then returned to New Zealand, where she taught at the University of Auckland for two years. In 1963 she accepted a position in the United States, at Carnegie-Mellon University in Pittsburgh. Ten years later she joined the faculty at the University of Pittsburgh, where she currently holds the position of Distinguished Service Professor. Baier serves on the editorial board of a number of philosophical journals and is a reader for several university presses. She has published many articles on the philosophy of mind, ethics, and the history of philosophy, some of which are collected in *Postures of the Mind* (1985). Baier is also the author of *Sentiments: Reflections on Hume's Treatise* (1991).

   Our reading is from Baier's 1985 article, "What Do Women Want in a Moral Theory?" Baier begins with a reference to Carol Gilligan's book *In a Different Voice*, published in 1982. Gilligan, a developmental psychologist at Harvard, points out that previous theories of human moral development are based mostly on studies of male subjects. Gilligan's research with female subjects, however, revealed patterns of moral thinking different from those in males. Women do not have the same moral attitudes as men; they speak "in a different voice." While males emphasize rules, obligation, justice, rights, and universality, females stress love, caring, cooperation, personal relationships, and the uniqueness of the situation. If Gilligan is right and women do have a substantially different moral vision than men, Baier asks, then what sort of moral theories would women produce?

   Baier briefly surveys recent writings of moral philosophers who are women. She finds these authors discussing topics such as love, mercy, honesty, relationships, the mistreatment of animals, and the destruction of the environment. But she finds none of them proposing a general moral *theory*. Baier states that the various points made by women moral philosophers could probably be unified into a single theory that has love as its fundamental principle. An ethic of love would qualify as a moral theory, but it would probably give too little scope to the moral principle that is central to the moral theories proposed by men: obligation. Baier asks whether there might be some higher concept that could include both love and obligation, providing a moral theory that embraces both feminine and masculine moral insights. She suggests that the concept of *trust* could serve this function. For, on the one hand, love requires that one trust others and be trustworthy; on the other hand, obligation involves entrusting others with the power to instill obligations, to require their fulfillment, and to impose sanctions if they go unfulfilled. The main question to be addressed by an ethic of trust would be: "Who should trust whom with what, and why?"

▼

When I finished reading Carol Gilligan's *In a Different Voice*,[1] I asked myself the obvious question for a philosopher reader, namely what differences

From Annette Baier, "What Do Women Want in a Moral Theory?" *Nous*, vol. 19, March, 1985, pp.43–63. © 1985. Used by permission of Blackwell Publishers and the author.

one should expect in the moral philosophy done by women, supposing Gilligan's sample of women representative, and supposing her analysis of their moral attitudes and moral development to be correct. Should one expect them to want to produce moral theories, and if so, what sort of moral theories? How will any moral theories they produce differ from those produced by men?

Obviously one does not have to make this an entirely a priori and hypothetical question. One can look and see what sort of contributions women have made to moral philosophy. Such a look confirms, I think, Gilligan's findings. What one finds *is* a bit different in tone and approach from the standard sort of moral philosophy as done by men following in the footsteps of the great moral philosophers (all men). Generalizations are extremely rash, but when I think of Philippa Foot's work on the moral virtues, of Elizabeth Anscombe's work on intention and on modern moral philosophy, of Iris Murdoch's philosophical writings, of Ruth Barcan Marcus' work on moral dilemmas, of the work of the radical feminist moral philosophers who are not content with orthodox Marxist lines of thought, of Jenny Teichman's book on illegitimacy, of Susan Wolf's recent articles, of Claudia Card's essay on mercy, Sabina Lovilbond's recent book, Gabriele Taylor's work on pride, love and on integrity, Cora Diamond's and Mary Midgley's work on our attitude to animals, Sissela Bok's work on lying and on secrecy, Virginia Held's work, the work of Alison Jaggar, Marilyn Frye, and many others, I seem to hear a different voice from the standard moral philosophers' voice. I hear the voice Gilligan heard, made reflective and philosophical. What women want in moral philosophy is what they are providing. And what they are providing seems to me to confirm Gilligan's theses about women. One has to be careful here, of course, for not all important contributions to moral philosophy by women fall easily into the Gilligan stereotype, nor its philosophical extension. Nor has it been only women who recently have been proclaiming discontent with the standard approach in moral philosophy, and trying new approaches. Michael Stocker, Alasdair MacIntyre, Ian Hacking when he assesses the game theoretic approach to morality,[2] all should be given the status of honorary women, if we accept the hypothesis that there are some moral insights which for whatever reason women seem to attain more easily or more reliably than men do. Still, exceptions confirm the rule, so I shall proceed undaunted by these important exceptions to my generalizations.

If Hacking is right, preoccupation with prisoner's and prisoners' dilemma is a big boys' game, and a pretty silly one too. It is, I think, significant that women have not rushed into the field of game-theoretic moral philosophy, and that those who have dared enter that male locker room have said distinctive things there. Edna Ullmann-Margalit's book *The Emergence of Norms*[3] put prisoners' dilemma in its limited moral place. Supposing that at least part of the explanation for the relatively few women in this field is disinclination rather than disability, one might ask if this disinclination also extends to a disinclination for the construction of moral theories. For although we find out what sort of moral philosophy women want by looking to see what they have provided, if we do that for moral theory, the answer we get seems to be "none." For none of the contributions to moral philosophy by women really count as moral theories, nor are seen as such by their authors.

Is it that reflective women, when they become philosophers, want to do without moral theory, want no part in the construction of such theories? To conclude this at this early stage, when we have only a few generations of women moral philosophers to judge from, would be rash indeed. The term "theory" can be used in wider and narrower ways, and in its widest sense a moral theory is simply an internally consistent fairly comprehensive account of what morality is and when and why it merits our acceptance and support. In that wide sense, a moral theory is something it would take a sceptic, or one who believes that our intellectual vision is necessarily blurred or distorted when we let it try to take in too much, to be an anti-theorist. Even if there were some truth in the latter claim, one might compatibly with it still hope to build up a coherent total account by a mosaic method, assembling a lot of smaller scale works until one had built up a complete account—say taking the virtues or purported virtues one by one until one had a more or less complete account. But would that sort of comprehensiveness in one's moral philosophy entitle one to call the finished work a moral theory? If it does, then many women moral philosophers today can be seen as engaged in moral theory construction. In the weakest sense of "theory," namely coherent near-comprehensive account, then there are plenty incomplete theories to be found in the works of women moral philosophers. And in *that* sense of theory, most of what are recognized as the current moral theories are also incomplete, since they do not purport to be yet really comprehensive. Wrongs to animals and wrongful destruction of our physical environment are put to one side by Rawls,[4] and in most "liberal" theories there are only hand waves concerning our proper attitude to our children, to the ill, to our relatives, friends and lovers.

Is comprehensiveness too much to ask of a moral theory? The paradigm examples of moral theories—those that are called by their authors "moral theories"—are distinguished not by the comprehensiveness of their internally coherent account, but by the *sort* of coherence which is aimed at over a fairly broad area. Their method is not the mosaic method, but the broad brushstroke method. Moral theories, as we know them, are, to change the art form, vaults rather than walls—they are not built by assembling painstakingly-made brick after brick. In *this* sense of theory, namely, fairly tightly systematic account of a fairly large area of morality, with a key stone supporting all the rest, women moral philosophers have not yet, to my knowledge, produced moral theories, nor claimed that they have.

Leaving to one side the question of what good purpose (other than good clean intellectual fun) is served by such moral theories, and supposing for the sake of argument that women can, if they wish, systematize as well as the next man, and if need be systematize in a mathematical fashion as well as the next mathematically minded moral philosopher, then what key concept, or guiding motif, might hold together the structure of a moral theory hypothetically produced by a reflective woman, Gilligan-style, who has taken up moral theorizing as a calling? What would be a suitable central question, principle, or concept, to structure a moral theory which might accommodate those moral insights women tend to have more readily than men, and to answer those moral questions which, it seems, worry women more than men? I hypothesized that the women's theory, expressive mainly of women's insights and concerns, would be an ethics of love, and this hypothesis seems to be Gilligan's too, since she has gone on from *In a Different Voice* to write about the limitations of Freud's understanding of love as women know it.[5] But presumably women theorists will be like enough to men to want their moral theory to be acceptable to all, so acceptable both to reflective women and to reflective men. Like any good theory, it will need not to ignore the partial truth of previous theories. So it must accommodate both the insights men have more easily than women, and those women have more easily than men. It should swallow up its predecessor theories. Women moral theorists, if any, will have this very great advantage over the men whose theories theirs supplant, that they can stand on the shoulders of men moral theorists, as no man has yet been able to stand on the shoulders of any woman moral theorist. There can be advantages, as well as handicaps, in being latecomers. So women theorists will need to connect their ethics of love with what has been the men theorists' preoccupation, namely obligation.

The great and influential moral theorists have in the modern era taken *obligation* as the key and the problematic concept, and have asked what justifies treating a person as morally bound or obliged to do a particular thing. Since to be bound is to be unfree, by making obligation central, one at the same time makes central the question of the justification of coercion, of forcing or trying to force someone to act in a particular way. The concept of obligation as justified limitation of freedom does just what one wants a good theoretical concept to do—to divide up the field (as one looks at different ways one's freedom may be limited, freedom in different spheres, different sorts and versions and levels of justification) and at the same time hold the subfields together. There must in a theory be some generalization and some speciation or diversification, and a good rich key concept guides one both in recognizing the diversity and in recognizing the unity in it. The concept of obligation has served this function very well for the area of morality it covers, and so we have some fine theories about that area. But as Aristotelians and Christians, as well as women, know, there is a lot of morality *not* covered by that concept, a lot of very great importance even for the area where there are obligations.[6]

This is fairly easy to see if we look at what lies behind the perceived obligation to keep promises. Unless there is some good moral reason why someone should assume the responsibility of rearing a child to be *capable* of taking promises seriously, once she understands what a promise is, the obligation to obey promises will not effectively tie her, and any force applied to punish her when she breaks promises or makes fraudulent ones will be of questionable justice. Is there an *obligation* on someone to make the child into a morally competent promisor? If so, on whom? Who have failed in their obligations when, say, war orphans who grew up without parental love or any other love arrive at legal adulthood very willing to be untrue to their word? Who failed in what obligation in all those less extreme cases of attempted but unsuccessful moral education? The parents who didn't produce promise-keeping offspring? Those who failed to educate the parents in how to educate their children (whoever it might be who might plausibly be thought to have the responsibility for training parents to fulfill their obligations)? The liberal version of our basic moral obligations tends to be fairly silent on who has what obligations to new members of the moral community, and it would throw most theories of the justification of obligations into some confusion if the obligation to lovingly rear one's children were added to the list of obligations. Such evidence as we have about the conditions in which children do successfully "learn" the morality of the community of which they are members suggests that we cannot substitute "conscientiously" for "lovingly" in this hypothetical extra needed obligation. But an obligation to love, in the strong sense needed, would be an embarrassment to the theorist, given most accepted versions of "ought implies can."

It is hard to make fair generalizations here, so I shall content myself with indicating how this charge I am making against the current men's moral theories, that their version of the justified list of obligations does not ensure the proper care of the young, so does nothing to ensure the stability of the morality in question over several generations, can be made against what I regard as the best of the men's recent theories, namely John Rawls' theory of justice. One of the great strengths of Rawls' theory is the careful attention given to the question of how just institutions produce the conditions for their continued support, across generations, and in particular of how the sense of justice will arise in children, once there are minimally just institutions structuring the social world into which they are born. Rawls, more than most moral theorists, has attended to the question of the stability of his just society, given what we know about child development. But Rawls' sensitive account of the conditions for the development of that sense of justice needed for the maintenance of his version of a just society takes it for granted that there will be loving parents rearing the children in whom the sense of justice is to develop. "The parents, we may suppose, love the child, and in time the child comes to love and trust the parents."[7] Why may we suppose this? Not because compliance with Rawls' version of our obligations and duties will ensure it. Rawls' theory, like so many other theories of obligation, in the end must take out a loan not only on the natural duty of parents to care for children (which he will have no trouble including), but on the natural *virtue* of parental love (or even a loan on the maternal instinct?). The virtue of being a *loving* parent must supplement the natural duties and the obligations of justice, if the just society is to last beyond the first generation. . . .

Granted that the men's theories of obligation need supplementation, to have much chance of integrity and coherence, and that the women's hypothetical theories will want to cover obligation as well as love, then what concept brings them together? My tentative answer is—the concept of appropriate trust, oddly neglected in moral theory. This concept also nicely mediates between reason and feeling, those tired old candidates for moral authority, since to trust is neither quite to believe something about the trusted, nor necessarily to feel any emotion towards them—but to have a belief-informed and action-influencing attitude. To make it plausible that the neglected concept of appropriate trust is a good one for the enlightened moral theorist to make central, I need to show, or begin to show, how it could include obligation, indeed shed light on obligations and their justification, as well as include love and the other moral concerns of Gilligan's women, and many of the topics women moral philosophers have chosen to address, mosaic fashion. I would also need to show that it could connect all of these in a way which holds out promise both of synthesis and of comprehensive moral coverage. A moral theory which looked at the conditions for proper trust of all the various sorts we show, and at what sorts of reasons justify inviting such trust, giving it, and meeting it, would, I believe, not have to avoid turning its gaze on the conditions for the survival of the practices it endorses, so it could avoid that unpleasant choice many current liberal theories seem to have—between incoherence and bad faith. I do not pretend that we will easily agree once we raise the questions I think we should raise, but at least we may have a language adequate to the expression of both men's and women's moral viewpoints.

My trust in the concept of trust is based in part on my own attempts to restate and consider what was right and what wrong with men's theories, especially Hume's,[8] which I consider the best of the lot. There I found myself reconstructing his account of the artifices of justice as an account of the progressive enlargement of a climate of trust, and found that a helpful way to see it. It has some textual basis, but is nevertheless a reconstruction, and one I found, immodestly, an improvement. So it is because I have tried the concept and explored its dimensions a bit—the variety of goods we may trust others not to take from us, the variety of sorts of security or insurance we have when we do, the sorts of defences or potential defences we lay down when we trust, the various conditions for reasonable trust of various types—that I am hopeful about its power as a theoretical not just an exegetical tool. I also found myself needing to use it, when I made a brief rash attempt at that women's topic, caring (invited in by a man philosopher,[9] I should say). That it does generalize some central moral features both of the recognition of binding obligations and moral virtues, and of loving, as well as of other important relations between persons, such as teacher-pupil, confider-confidante, worker to co-worker in the same cause, professional to client, I am reasonably sure. Indeed it is fairly obvious that love, the main moral phenomenon women want attended to, involves trust, so I anticipate little quarrel when I claim that, if we had a moral theory spelling out the conditions for appropriate trust and distrust, that would include a morality of love in all its variants—parental love, love of children for their parents, love of family members, love of friends, of lovers in the strict sense, of co-workers, of one's country and its figureheads, of exemplary heroines and heros, of goddesses and gods.

Love and loyalty demand maximal trust of one sort, and maximal trustworthiness, and in investigating the conditions for maximal trust and maximal risk we must think about the ethics of love. More controversial may be my claim that the ethics of obligation will also be covered. I see it as covered since to recognize a set of obligations is to trust some group of persons to instill them, to demand that they be met, possibly to levy sanctions if they are not, and this is to trust persons with very significant coercive power over others. Less coercive but still significant power is possessed by those shaping our conception of the virtues, and expecting us to display them, approving when we do, disapproving and perhaps shunning us when we do not. Such coercive and manipulative power over others requires justification, and is justified only if we have reason to trust those who have it to use it properly, and to use the discretion which is always given when trust is given in a way which serves the purpose of the whole system of moral control, and not merely self-serving or morally improper purposes. Since the question of the justification of coercion becomes, at least in part, the question of the wisdom of trusting the coercers to do their job properly, the morality of obligation, inasfar as it reduces to the morality of coercion, is covered by the morality of proper trust. Other forms of trust may also be involved, but trusting enforcers with the use of force is the most problematic form of trust involved.

The coercers and manipulators are, to some extent, all of us, so to ask what our obligations are and what virtues we should exhibit is to ask what it is reasonable to trust us to demand, expect, and contrive to get, from one another. It becomes, in part, a question of what powers we can in reason trust ourselves to exercise properly. But self-trust is a dubious or limited case of trust, so I prefer to postpone the examination of the concept of proper self-trust at least until proper trust of others is more clearly understood. Nor do we distort matters too much if we concentrate on those cases where moral sanctions and moral pressure and moral manipulation is not self-applied but applied to others, particularly by older persons to younger persons. Most moral pressuring that has any effects goes on in childhood and early youth. Moral sanctions may continue to be applied, formally and informally, to adults, but unless the criminal courts apply them it is easy enough for adults to ignore them, to brush them aside. It is not difficult to become a sensible knave, and to harden one's heart so that one is insensible to the moral condemnation of one's victims and those who sympathize with them. Only if the pressures applied in the morally formative stage have given one a heart that rebels against the thought of such ruthless independence of what others think will one see any reason *not* to ignore moral condemnation, not to treat it as mere powerless words and breath. Condemning sensible knaves is as much a waste of breath as arguing with them—all we can sensibly do is to try to protect children against their influence, and ourselves against their knavery. Adding to the criminal law will not be the way to do the latter, since such moves will merely challenge sensible knaves to find new knavish exceptions and loopholes, not protect us from sensible knavery. Sensible knaves are precisely those who exploit us without breaking the law. So the whole question of when moral pressure of various sorts, formative, reformative, and punitive, ought to be brought to bear by whom is subsumed under the question of whom to trust when and with what, and for what good reasons.

In concentrating on obligations rather than virtues, modern moral theorists have chosen to look at the cases where more trust is placed in enforcers of obligations than is placed in ordinary moral agents, the bearers of the obligations. In taking, as contractarians do, contractual obligations as the model of obligations, they concentrate on a case where the very minimal trust is put in the obligated person, and considerable punitive power entrusted to the one to whom the obligation is owed (I assume here that Hume is right in saying that when we promise or contract, we formally subject ourselves to the penalty, in case of failure, of never being trusted as a promisor again). This is an interesting case of the allocation of trust of various sorts, but it surely distorts our moral vision to suppose that *all* obligations, let alone all morally pressured expectations we impose on others, conform to that abnormally coercive model. It takes very special conditions for it to be safe to trust persons to inflict penalties on other persons, conditions in which either we can trust the penalizers to have the virtues necessary to penalize wisely and fairly, or else we can rely on effective threats to keep unvirtuous penalizers from abusing their power—that is to say, rely on others to coerce the first coercers into proper behaviour. But that reliance too will either be trust, or will have to rely on threats from coercers of the coercers of coercers, and so on. Morality on this model becomes a nasty, if intellectually intriguing, game of mutual mutually corrective threats. The central question of who should deprive whom of what freedom soon becomes the question of whose anger should be dreaded by whom (the theory of obligation) supplemented perhaps by an afterthought on whose favor should be courted by whom (the theory of the virtues).

Undoubtedly some important part of morality does depend in part on a system of threats and bribes, at least for its survival in difficult conditions when normal goodwill and normally virtuous dispositions may be insufficient to motivate the conduct required for the preservation and justice of the moral network of relationships. But equally undoubtedly life will be nasty, emotionally poor, and worse than brutish (even if longer), if that is all morality is, or even if that coercive structure of morality is regarded as the backbone, rather than as an available crutch, should the main support fail. For the main support has to come from those we entrust with the job of rearing and training persons so that they can be trusted in various ways, some trusted with extraordinary coercive powers, some with public decision-making powers, all trusted as parties to promise, most trusted by some who love them and by one or more willing to become co-parents with them, most trusted by dependent children, dependent elderly relatives, sick friends, and so on. A very complex network of a great variety of sorts of trust structures our moral relationships with our fellows, and if there is a *main* support to this network, it is the trust we place in those who respond to the trust of new members of the moral community, namely of children, and prepare them for new forms of trust.

A theory which took as its central question "Who should trust whom with what, and why?" would not have to forego the intellectual fun and games previous theorists have had with the various paradoxes of morality—curbing freedom to increase freedom, curbing self-interest the better to satisfy self-interest, not aiming at happiness in order to become happier. For it is easy enough to get a paradox of trust to accompany or, if I am right, to generalize the paradoxes of freedom, self-interest and hedonism. To trust is to make oneself or let oneself be more vulnerable than one might have been to harm from others—to give them an opportunity to harm one, in the confidence that they will not take it, because they have no good reason to. Why would one take such a risk? For risk it always is, given the partial opaqueness to us of the reasoning and motivation of those we trust and with whom we cooperate. Our confidence may be, and quite often is, misplaced. That is what we risk when we trust. If the best reason to take such a risk is the expected gain in security which comes from a climate of trust, then in trusting we are always giving up security to get greater security, exposing our throats so that others become accustomed to not biting. A moral theory which made proper trust its central concern could have its own categorical imperative,[10] could replace obedience to self-made laws and freely chosen restraint on freedom with security-increasing sacrifice of security, distrust in the promoters of a climate of distrust, and so on.

Such reflexive use of one's central concept, negative or affirmative, is an intellectually satisfying activity which is bound to have appeal to those system-lovers who want to construct moral theories, and it may help them design their theory in an intellectually pleasing manner. But we should beware of becoming hypnotized by our slogans, or of sacrificing truth to intellectual elegance. Any theory of proper trust should not *prejudge* the question of when distrust is proper. We might find more objects of proper distrust than just the contributors to a climate of reasonable distrust, just as freedom should be restricted not just to increase human freedom but to protect human life from poisoners and other killers. I suspect, however, that all the objects of reasonable distrust are more reasonably seen as falling into the category of ones who contribute to a decrease in the scope of proper trust, than can all who are reasonably coerced be seen as themselves guilty of wrongful coercion. Still, even if all proper trust turns out to be for such persons and on such matters as will increase the scope or stability of a climate of reasonable trust, and all proper distrust for such persons and on such matters as increase the scope of reasonable distrust, overreliance on such nice reflexive formulae can distract us from asking all the questions about trust which need to be asked, if an adequate moral theory is to be constructed around that concept. These questions should include when to *respond* to trust with *un*trustworthiness, when and when not to invite trust, as well as when to give and refuse trust. We should not assume that promiscuous trustworthiness is any more a virtue than is undiscriminating distrust. It is appropriate trustworthiness, appropriate trustingness, appropriate encouragement to trust, which will be virtues, as will be judicious untrustworthiness, selective refusal to trust, discriminating discouragement of trust.

Women are particularly well placed to appreciate these last virtues, since they have sometimes needed them to get into a position to even consider becoming moral theorizers. The long exploitation and domination of women by men depended on men's trust in women and women's trustworthiness to play their allotted role and so to perpetuate their own and their daughters' servitude. However keen women now are to end the lovelessness of modern moral philosophy, they are unlikely to lose sight of the cautious virtue of appropriate distrust, or of the tough virtue of principled betrayal of the exploiters' trust.

Gilligan's girls and women saw morality as a matter of preserving valued ties to others, of preserving the conditions for that care and mutual care without which human life becomes bleak, lonely, and after a while, as the mature men in her study found, not self-affirming, however successful in achieving the egoistic goals which had been set. The boys and men saw morality as a matter of finding workable traffic rules for self-assertors, so that they not needlessly frustrate one another, and so that they could, should they so choose, cooperate in more positive ways to mutual advantage. Both for the women's sometimes unchosen and valued ties with others, and for the men's mutual respect as sovereigns and subjects of the same minimal moral traffic rules (and for their more voluntary and more selective associations of profiteers), trust is important. Both men and women are concerned with cooperation, and the dimensions of trust-distrust structure the different cooperative relations each emphasize. The various considerations which arise when we try to defend an answer to any question about the appropriateness of a particular form of cooperation with its distinctive form of trust or distrust, that is, when we look into the terms of all sorts of cooperation, at the terms of trust in different cases of trust, at what are fair terms and what are trust-enhancing and trust-preserving terms, are suitably many and richly interconnected. A moral theory (or family of theories) that made trust its central problem could do better justice to men's and women's moral intuitions than do the going men's theories. Even if we don't easily agree on the answer to the question of who should trust whom with what, who should accept and who should meet various sorts of trust, and why, these questions might enable us better to morally reason together than we can when the central moral questions are reduced to those of whose favor one must court and whose anger one must dread. But such programmatic claims as I am making will be tested only when women standing on the shoulders of men, or men on the shoulders of women, or some theorizing Tiresias,[11] actually work out such a theory. I am no Tiresias, and have not foresuffered all the labor pains of such a theory. I aim here only to fertilize.

▶ NOTES

1. Cambridge, Mass.: Harvard University Press, 1982. [D.C.A., ed.]
2. Ian Hacking, "Winner Takes Less," a review of *The Evolution of Cooperation* by Robert Axelrod, *New York Review of Books,* June 28, 1984. [A.C.B.] The "game theoretic" approach to morality compares situations requiring moral decisions to games in which individuals try to maximize their self-interest. The most discussed example is the "prisoners' dilemma," which Baier mentions in the following paragraph. In this imaginary dilemma, two prisoners guilty of a crime are interrogated separately. Both prisoners know (1) that if *neither* confesses, they will both get rather light sentences; (2) that if one confesses and the other does not, the one who confesses will fare best (by turning state's evidence) and the one who does not will fare worst (by receiving a vindictive sentence); and (3) that if they *both* confess, they will both avoid the worst but neither will attain the best. Each prisoner faces the dilemma of whether to confess or not. [D.C.A.]
3. Oxford, England: Clarendon Press, 1977. [D.C.A.]
4. John Rawls, *A Theory of Justice* (Cambridge, Mass.: Harvard University Press, 1971). [D.C.A.]
5. "The Conquistador and the Dark Continent: Reflections on the Psychology of Love," *Daedalus,* Summer 1984. [A.C.B.]
6. The following two paragraphs were not included in the version of the article published in *Noûs* (Vol. 19, March 1985, pp. 53–63); they were supplied by Professor Baier for use here and are reprinted with her kind permission. These two paragraphs form part of a longer section

omitted from the *Noûs* version. The complete version of the article will appear in Baier's forthcoming collection, *Moral Prejudices.* [D.C.A.]

7. Rawls, *A Theory of Justice,* p. 463. [D.C.A.]

8. David Hume (1711–1776) was a Scottish philosopher and historian. [D.C.A.]

9. "Caring About Caring," a response to Harry Frankfurt's "What We Care About," both in *Matters of the Mind, Synthese* 53 (November 1982): 257–290. [A.C.B.] Baier's article is reprinted in her collection *Postures of the Mind* (Minneapolis: University of Minnesota Press, 1985). [D.C.A.]

10. *categorical imperative:* an unconditionally binding moral command. The term comes from the German philosopher Immanuel Kant (1724–1804). [D.C.A.]

11. Tiresias was a legendary blind seer of the ancient Greek city of Thebes. [D.C.A.]

Feminism and Moral Theory

Virginia Held

Virginia Held was born in Mendham, New Jersey, in 1929. She attended Barnard
College of Columbia University, receiving her bachelor's degree in philosophy in 1950.
After pursuing graduate studies in France for a year with a Fulbright Grant, she gave up
philosophy for a decade because it seemed too remote from the social and political
problems that had become her central concerns. Held worked for a magazine of news
and opinion, doing research and occasional writing. But after seeing how philosophical
assumptions pervaded the thinking of those outside academics, she resumed graduate
studies in philosophy, completing her doctorate at Columbia in 1968. Held has been
teaching at Hunter College of the City University of New York since 1965. Since 1977
she has also been on the faculty of the Graduate School of the City University of New
York. Held has been a visiting professor at Yale University, Dartmouth College, the
University of California at Los Angeles, and Hamilton College. She has also been a visiting scholar at Harvard Law School.

Held's works, which have contributed to the renewed philosophical interest in
applied ethics, include *The Public Interest and Individual Interests* (1970), *Property, Profits,
and Economic Justice* (editor, 1980), *Rights and Goods: Justifying Social Action* (1984), and
Feminist Morality: Transforming Culture, Society, and Politics (1993; an expansion of the
moral theory outlined in our reading).

Our reading is from Held's 1987 article, "Women and Moral Theory." Held first
states her belief that philosophers should postpone their attempts to devise a general
moral theory covering all domains of human activity and should instead devote their
energies to developing theories for specific, actual contexts. Her article explores ethical issues pertaining to the context of a large part of many women's experience: motherhood.

Held argues that ethical theories that view contractual exchange as the fundamental social relationship are suitable for the activity of commerce, but inappropriate for
the family. She contends that the foundation of society is the mother-child relation, not
the buyer-seller relation of the marketplace, and that the nurturing relationship (the
nurturer need not be the mother) may turn out to be the paradigm for all human relationships.

An ethics focused on nurture would help turn our ethical attention away from the
two poles of *self* and *all others,* and toward the intermediate region of "particular others"
(for example, relatives and friends). Such an ethics would put less emphasis on general
moral principles but not eliminate them altogether. Held concludes by exploring the
significance for moral theory of the fact that, although both men and women can nurture children, only women can give birth.

▼

The tasks of moral inquiry and moral practice are such that different moral
approaches may be appropriate for different domains of human activity. I
have argued in a recent book[1] that we need a division of moral labor. In
Rights and Goods, I suggest that we ought to try to develop moral inquiries
that will be as satisfactory as possible for the actual contexts in which we live

. . . . . .

and in which our experience is located. Such a division of moral labor can be expected to yield different moral theories for different contexts of human activity, at least for the foreseeable future. In my view, the moral approaches most suitable for the courtroom are not those most suitable for political bargaining; the moral approaches suitable for economic activity are not those suitable for relations within the family, and so on. The task of achieving a unified moral field theory covering all domains is one we may do well to postpone, while we do our best to devise and to "test" various moral theories in actual contexts and in light of our actual moral experience.

What are the implications of such a view for women? Traditionally, the experience of women has been located to a large extent in the context of the family. In recent centuries, the family has been thought of as a "private" domain distinct not only from that of the "public" domain of the polis,[2] but also from the domain of production and of the marketplace. Women (and men) certainly need to develop moral inquiries appropriate to the context of mothering and of family relations, rather than accepting the application to this context of theories developed for the marketplace or the polis. We can certainly show that the moral guidelines appropriate to mothering are different from those that now seem suitable for various other domains of activity as presently constituted. But we need to do more as well: we need to consider whether distinctively feminist moral theories, suitable for the contexts in which the experience of women has or will continue to be located, are better moral theories than those already available, and better for other domains as well. . . .

Mothering and Markets

When we bring women's experience fully into the domain of moral consciousness, we can see how questionable it is to imagine contractual relationships as central or fundamental to society and morality. They seem, instead, the relationships of only very particular regions of human activity.

The most central and fundamental social relationship seems to be that between mother or mothering person and child. It is this relationship that creates and recreates society. It is the activity of mothering which transforms biological entities into human social beings. Mothers and mothering persons produce children and empower them with language and symbolic representations. Mothers and mothering persons thus produce and create human culture.

Despite its implausibility, the assumption is often made that human mothering is like the mothering of other animals rather than being distinctively human. In accordance with the traditional distinction between the family and the polis, and the assumption that what occurs in the public sphere of the polis is distinctively human, it is assumed that what human mothers do within the family belongs to the "natural" rather than to the "distinctively human" domain. Or, if it is recognized that the activities of human mothers do not resemble the activities of the mothers of other mammals, it is assumed that, at least, the difference is far narrower than the difference between what animals do and what humans who take part in government and industry and art do. But, in fact, mothering is among the most human of human activities.

Consider the reality. A human birth is thoroughly different from the birth of other animals, because a human mother can choose not to give birth. However extreme the alternative, even when abortion is not a possibility, a woman can choose suicide early enough in her pregnancy to consciously prevent the birth. A human mother comprehends that she brings about the birth of another human being. A human mother is then responsible, at least in an existentialist sense, for the creation of a new human life. The event is essentially different from what is possible for other animals.

Human mothering is utterly different from the mothering of animals without language. The human mother or nurturing person constructs with and for the child a human social reality. The child's understanding of language and of symbols, and of all that they create and make real, occurs in interactions between child and caretakers. Nothing seems more distinctively human than this. In comparison, government can be thought to resemble the governing of ant colonies, industrial production to be similar to the building of beaver dams, a market exchange to be like the relation between a large fish that protects and a small fish that grooms, and the conquest by force of arms that characterizes so much of human history to be like the aggression of packs of animals. But the imparting of language and the creation within and for each individual of a human social reality, and often a new human social reality, seems utterly human.

An argument is often made that art and industry and government create new human reality, while mothering merely "reproduces" human beings, their cultures, and social structures. But consider a more accurate view: in bringing up children, those who mother create new human *persons*. They change persons, the culture, and the social structures that depend on them, by creating the kinds of persons who can continue to transform themselves and their surroundings. Creating new and better persons is surely as "creative" as creating new and better objects or institutions. It is not only bodies that do not spring into being unaided and fully formed; neither do imaginations, personalities, and minds.

Perhaps morality should make room first for the human experience reflected in the social bond between mothering person and child, and for the human projects of nurturing and of growth apparent for both persons in the relationship. In comparison, the transactions of the marketplace seem peripheral; the authority of weapons and the laws they uphold, beside the point.

The relation between buyer and seller has often been taken as the model of all human interactions. Most of the social contract tradition has seen this relation of contractual exchange as fundamental to law and political authority as well as to economic activity. And some contemporary moral philosophers see the contractual relation as the relation on which even morality itself should be based. The marketplace, as a model for relationships, has become so firmly entrenched in our normative theories that it is rarely questioned as a proper foundation for recommendations extending beyond the marketplace. Consequently, much moral thinking is built on the concept of rational economic man. Relationships between human beings are seen as arising, and as justified, when they serve the interests of individual rational contractors.

In the society imagined in the model based on assumptions about rational economic man, connections between people become no more than instrumental. Nancy Hartsock effectively characterizes the worldview of these assumptions, and shows how misguided it is to suppose that the relationship between buyer and seller can serve as a model for all human relations: "the paradigmatic connections between people [on this view of the social world] are instrumental or extrinsic and conflictual, and in a world populated by these isolated individuals, relations of competition and domination come to be substitutes for a more substantial and encompassing community."[3]

Whether the relationship between nurturing person (who need not be a biological mother) and child should be taken as itself paradigmatic, in place of the contractual paradigm, or whether it should be seen only as an obviously important relationship that does not fit into the contractual framework and should not be overlooked, remains to be seen. It is certainly instructive to consider it, at least tentatively, as paradigmatic. If this were done, the competition and desire for domination thought of as acceptable for rational economic man might appear as a very particular and limited human connection, suitable perhaps, if at all, only for a restricted marketplace. Such a relation of conflict and competition can be seen to be unacceptable for establishing the social trust on which public institutions must rest, or for upholding the bonds on which caring, regard, friendship, or love must be based.

The social map would be fundamentally altered by adoption of the point of view here suggested. Possibly, the relationship between "mother" and child would be recognized as a much more promising source of trust and concern than any other, for reasons to be explored later. In addition, social relations would be seen as dynamic rather than as fixed-point exchanges. And assumptions that human beings are equally capable of entering or not entering into the contractual relations taken to characterize social relations generally would be seen for the distortions they are. Although human mothers could do other than give birth, their choices to do so or not are usually highly constrained. And children, even human children, cannot choose at all whether to be born.

It may be that no human relationship should be thought of as paradigmatic for all the others. Relations between mothering persons and children can become oppressive for both, and relations between equals who can decide whether to enter into agreements may seem attractive in contrast. But no mapping of the social and moral landscape can possibly be satisfactory if it does not adequately take into account and provide appropriate guidance for relationships between mothering persons and children.

Between the Self and the Universal

Perhaps the most important legacy of the new insights will be the recognition that more attention must be paid to the domain *between* the self—the ego, the self-interested individual—on the one hand, and the universal—everyone, others in general—on the other hand. Ethics traditionally has dealt with these poles, trying to reconcile their conflicting claims. It has called for impartiality against the partiality of the egoistic self, or it has defended the claims of egoism against such demands for a universal perspective.

In seeing the problems of ethics as problems of reconciling the interests of the self with what would be right or best for everyone, moral theory has neglected the intermediate region of family relations and relations of friendship, and has neglected the sympathy and concern people actually feel for particular others. As Larry Blum has shown, "contemporary moral philosophy in the Anglo-American tradition has paid little attention to [the] morally significant phenomena" of sympathy, compassion, human concern, and friendship.[4]

Standard moral philosophy has construed personal relationships as aspects of the self-interested feelings of individuals, as when a person might favor those he loves over those distant because it satisfies his own desires to do so. Or it has let those close others stand in for the universal "other," as when an analysis might be offered of how the conflict between self and others is to be resolved in something like "enlightened self-interest" or "acting out of respect for the moral law," and seeing this as what should guide us in our relations with those close, particular others with whom we interact. . . .

The region of "particular others" is a distinct domain, where it can be seen that what becomes artificial and problematic are the very "self" and "all others" of standard moral theory. In the domain of particular others, the self is already closely entwined in relations with others, and the relation may be much more real, salient, and important than the interests of any individual self in isolation. But the "others" in the picture are not "all others," or "everyone," or what a universal point of view could provide. They are particular flesh and blood others for whom we have actual feelings in our insides and in our skin, not the others of rational constructs and universal principles.

Relationships can be characterized as trusting or mistrustful, mutually considerate or selfish, and so forth. Where trust and consideration are appropriate, we can find ways to foster them. But doing so will depend on aspects of what can be understood only if we look at relations between persons. To focus on either self-interested individuals or the totality of all persons is to miss the qualities of actual relations between actual human beings.

Moral theories must pay attention to the neglected realm of particular others in actual contexts. In doing so, problems of egoism vs. the universal moral point of view appear very different, and may recede to the region of background insolubility or relative unimportance. The important problems may then be seen to be how we ought to guide or maintain or reshape the relationships, both close and more distant, that we have or might have with actual human beings.

Particular others can, I think, be actual starving children in Africa with whom one feels empathy or even the anticipated children of future generations, not just those we are close to in any traditional context of family, neighbors, or friends. But particular others are still not "all rational beings" or "the greatest number."

In recognizing the component of feeling and relatedness between self and particular others, motivation is addressed as an inherent part of moral inquiry. Caring between parent and child is a good example. We should not glamorize parental care. Many mothers and fathers dominate their children in harmful or inappropriate ways, or fail to care adequately for them. But when the relationship between "mother" and child is as it should be, the caretaker does not care for the child (nor the child for the caretaker) because of universal moral rules. The love and concern one feels for the child already motivate much of what one does. This is not to say that morality is irrelevant. One must still decide what one ought to do. But the process of addressing the moral questions in mothering and of trying to arrive at answers one can find acceptable involves motivated acting, not just thinking. And neither egoism nor a morality of universal rules will be of much help. . . .

The feelings characteristic of mothering—that there are too many demands on us, that we cannot do everything that we ought to do—are highly instructive. They give rise to problems different from those of universal rule vs. self-interest. They require us to weigh the claims of one self-other relationship against the claims of other self-other relationships, to try to bring about some harmony between them, to see the issues in an actual temporal context, and to act rather than merely reflect.

For instance, we have limited resources for caring. We cannot care for everyone or do everything a caring approach suggests. We need moral guidelines for ordering our priorities. The hunger of our own children comes before the hunger of children we do not know. But the hunger of children in Africa ought to come before some of the expensive amusements we may wish to provide for our own children. These are moral problems calling to some extent for principled answers. But we have to figure out what we ought to do when actually buying groceries, cooking meals, refusing the requests of our children for the latest toy they have seen advertised, and sending money to UNICEF. The context is one of real action, not of ideal thought.

Principles and Particulars

When we take the context of mothering as central, rather than peripheral, for moral theory, we run the risk of excessively discounting other contexts. It is a commendable risk, given the enormously more prevalent one of excessively discounting mothering. But I think that the attack on principles has sometimes been carried too far by critics of traditional moral theory.

Noddings, for instance, writes that "To say, 'It is wrong to cause pain needlessly,' contributes nothing by way of knowledge and can hardly be thought likely to change the attitude or behavior of one who might ask, 'Why is it wrong?' . . . Ethical caring . . . depends not upon rule or principle" but upon the development of a self "in congruence with one's best remembrance of caring and being cared-for."[5]

We should not forget that an absence of principles can be an invitation to capriciousness. Caring may be a weak defense against arbitrary decisions, and the person cared for may find the relation more satisfactory if both persons, but especially the person caring, are guided, to some extent, by principles concerning obligations and rights. To argue that no two cases are ever alike is to invite moral chaos. Furthermore, for one person to be in a position of caretaker means that that person has the power to withhold care, to leave the other without it. The person cared for is usually in a position of vulnerability. The moral significance of this needs to be addressed along with other aspects of the caring relationship. Principles may remind a giver of questions, for instance those of economic justice. Such issues cry out for relevant principles. Although caring may be needed to motivate us to act on such principles, the principles are not dispensable. Noddings questions the concern people may have for starving persons in distant countries, because she sees universal love and universal justice as masculine illusions. She refrains from judging that the rich deserve less or the poor more, because caring for individuals cannot yield such judgments. But this may amount to taking a given economic stratification as given, rather than as the appropriate object of critical scrutiny that it should be. It may lead to accepting that the rich will care for the rich and the poor for the poor, with the gap between them, however unjustifiably wide, remaining what it is. Some important moral issues seem beyond the reach of an ethic of caring, once caring leads us, perhaps through empathy, to be concerned with them.

On ethical views that renounce principles as excessively abstract, we might have few arguments to uphold the equality of women. After all, as parents can care for children recognized as weaker, less knowledgeable, less capable, and with appropriately restricted rights, so men could care for women deemed inferior in every way. On a view that ethics could satisfactorily be founded on caring alone, men could care for women considered undeserving of equal rights in all the significant areas in which women have been struggling to have their equality recognized. So an ethic of care, essential as a component of morality, seems deficient if taken as an exclusive preoccupation.

That aspect of the attack on principles which seems entirely correct is the view that not all ethical problems can be solved by appeal to one or a very few simple principles. It is often argued that all more particular moral rules or principles can be derived from such underlying ones as the categorical imperative or the principle of utility,[6] and that these can be applied to all moral problems. The call for an ethic of care may be a call, which I share, for a more pluralistic view of ethics, recognizing that we need a division of moral labor employing different moral approaches for different domains, at least for the time being. Satisfactory intermediate principles for areas such as those of international affairs, or family relations, cannot be derived from simple universal principles, but must be arrived at in conjunction with experience within the domains in question.

Attention to particular others will always require that we respect the particularity of the context, and arrive at solutions to moral problems that will not give moral principles more weight than their due. But their due may remain considerable. And we will need principles concerning relationships, not only concerning the actions of individuals, as we will need evaluations of kinds of relationships, not only of the character traits of individuals.

Birth and Valuing

To a large extent, the activity of mothering is potentially open to men as well as to women. Fathers can conceivably come to be as emotionally close, or as close through caretaking, to children as are mothers. The experience of relatedness, of responsibility for the growth and empowerment of new life, and of responsiveness to particular others, ought to be incorporated into moral theory, and will have to be so incorporated for moral theory to be adequate. At present, in this domain, it is primarily the experience of women (and of children) that has not been sufficiently reflected in moral theory and that ought to be so reflected. But this is not to say that it must remain experience available only to women. If men came to share fully and equitably in the care of all persons who need care—especially children, the sick, the old—the moral values that now arise for women in the context of caring might arise as fully for men.

There are some experiences, however, that are open only to women: menstruating, having an abortion, giving birth, suckling. We need to consider their possible significance or lack of significance for moral experience and theory. I will consider here only one kind of experience not open to men but of obviously great importance to women: the experience of giving birth or of deciding not to. Does the very experience of giving birth, or of deciding not to exercise the capacity to do so, make a significant difference for moral experience and moral theory? I think the answer must be: perhaps.

Of course birthing is a social as well as a personal or biological event. It takes place in a social context structured by attitudes and arrangements that deeply affect how women experience it: whether it will be accepted as "natural," whether it will be welcomed and celebrated, or whether it will be fraught with fear or shame. But I wish to focus briefly on the conscious awareness women can have of what they are doing in giving birth, and on the specifically personal and biological aspects of human birthing.

It is women who give birth to other persons. Women are responsible for the existence of new persons in ways far more fundamental than are men. It is not bizarre to recognize that women can, through abortion or suicide, choose not to give birth. A woman can be aware of the possibility that she can act to prevent a new person from existing, and can be aware that if this new person exists, it is because of what she has done and made possible. . . .

Of all the human capacities, it is probably the capacity to create new human beings that is most worth celebrating. We can expect that a woman will care about and feel concern for a child she has created as the child grows and develops, and that she feels responsible for having given the child life. But her concern is more than something to be expected. It is, perhaps, justifiable in certain ways unique to women.

Children are born into actual situations. A mother cannot escape ultimate responsibility for having given birth to this particular child in these particular circumstances. She can be aware that she could have avoided intercourse, or used more effective contraception, or waited to get pregnant until her circumstances were different; that she could have aborted this child and had another later; or that she could have killed herself and prevented this child from facing the suffering or hardship of this particular life. The momentousness of all these decisions about giving or not giving life can hardly fail to affect what she experiences in relation to the child. . . .

Perhaps there is a tendency to want to approve of or to justify what one has decided with respect to giving life. In deciding to give birth, perhaps a woman has a natural tendency to approve of the birth, to believe that the child ought to have been born. Perhaps this inclines her to believe whatever may follow from this: that the child is entitled to care, and that feelings of love for the child are appropriate and justified. The conscious decision to create a new human being may provide women with an inclination to value the child and to have hope for the child's future. Since, in her view, the child ought to have been born, a woman may feel that the world ought to be hospitable to the child. And if the child ought to have been born, the child ought to grow into an admirable human adult. The child's life has, and should continue to have, value that is recognized.

Consider next the phenomenon of sacrifice. In giving birth, women suffer severe pain for the sake of new life. Having suffered for the child in giving the child life, women may have a natural tendency to value what they have endured pain for. There is a tendency, often noted in connection with war, for people to feel that because sacrifices have been made, the sacrifice should have been "worth it," and if necessary, other things ought to be done so that the sacrifice "shall not have been in vain." There may be a similar tendency for those who have suffered to give birth to assure themselves that the pain was for the good reason of creating a new life that is valuable and that will be valued.

Certainly, this is not to say that there is anything good or noble about suffering, or that merely because people want to believe that what they suffered for was worthwhile, it was. A vast amount of human suffering has been in vain, and could and should have been avoided. The point is that once suffering has already occurred and the "price," if we resort to such calculations, has already been paid, it will be worse if the result is a further cost, and better if the result is a clear benefit that can make the price, when it is necessary for the result, validly "worth it."

The suffering of the mother who has given birth will more easily have been worthwhile if the child's life has value. The chance that the suffering will be outweighed by future happiness is much greater if the child is valued by the society and the family into which the child is born. If the mother's suffering yields nothing but further suffering and a being deemed to be of no value, her suffering may truly have been in vain. Anyone can have reasons to value children. But the person who has already undergone the suffering needed to create one has a special reason to recognize that the child is valuable and to want the child to be valued so that the suffering she has already borne will have been, truly, worthwhile.

These arguments can be repeated for the burdens of work and anxiety normally expended in bringing up a child. Those who have already borne these burdens have special reasons for wanting to see the grown human being for whom they have cared as valuable and valued. Traditionally, women have not only borne the burdens of childbirth, but, with little help, the much greater burdens of child rearing. Of course, the burdens of child rearing could be shared fully by men, as they have been partially shared by women other than natural mothers. Although the concerns involved in bringing up a child may greatly outweigh the suffering of childbirth itself, this does not mean that giving birth is incidental.

The decision not to have children is often influenced by a comparable tendency to value the potential child. Knowing how much care the child would deserve and how highly, as a mother, she would value the child, a woman who gives up the prospect of motherhood can recognize how much she is losing. For such reasons, a woman may feel overwhelming ambivalence concerning the choice.

Consider, finally, how biology can affect our ways of valuing children. Although men and women may share a desire or an instinctive tendency to wish to reproduce, and although these feelings may be equally strong for both men and women, such feelings might affect their attitudes toward a given child very differently. In terms of biological capacity, a mother has a relatively greater stake in a child to which she has given birth. This child is about one-twentieth or one twenty-fifth of all the children she could possibly have, whereas a man could potentially have hundreds or thousands of other children. In giving birth, a woman has already contributed a large amount of energy and effort toward the production of this particular child, while a man has, biologically, contributed only a few minutes. To the extent that such biological facts may influence attitudes, the attitudes of the mother and father toward the "worth" or "value" of a particular child may be different. The father might consider the child more easily replaceable in the sense that the father's biological contribution can so easily and so painlessly be repeated on another occasion or with another woman; for the mother to repeat her biological contribution would be highly exhausting and painful. The mother, having already contributed so much more to the creation of this particular child than the father, might value the result of her effort in proportion. And her pride at what she has accomplished in giving birth can be appropriately that much greater. She has indeed "accomplished" far more than has the father. . . .

Morality and Human Tendencies

So far, I have been describing possible feelings rather than attaching any moral value to them. That children are valued does not mean that they are valuable, and if mothers have a natural tendency to value their children, it does not follow that they ought to. But if feelings are taken to be relevant to moral theory, the feelings of valuing the child, like the feelings of empathy for other persons in pain, may be of moral significance.

To the extent that a moral theory takes natural male tendencies into account, it would at least be reasonable to take natural female tendencies into account. Traditional moral theories often suppose it is legitimate for individuals to maximize self-interest, or satisfy their preferences, within certain constraints based on the equal rights of others. If it can be shown that the tendency to want to pursue individual self-interest is a stronger tendency among men than among women, this would certainly be relevant to an evaluation of such theory. And if it could be shown that a tendency to value children and a desire to foster the developing capabilities of the particular others for whom we care is a stronger tendency among women than among men, this too would be relevant in evaluating moral theories.

Many moral theories, and fields dependent on them such as economics, employ the assumption that to increase the utility[7] of individuals is a good thing to do. But if asked *why* it is a good thing to increase utility, or satisfy desire, or produce pleasure, or *why* doing so counts as a good reason for something, it is very difficult to answer. The claim is taken as a kind of starting assumption for which no *further* reason can be given. It seems to rest on a view that people seek pleasure, or that we can recognize pleasure as having intrinsic value. But if women recognize quite different assumptions as more likely to be valid, that would certainly be of importance to ethics. We might then take it as one of our starting assumptions that creating good relations of care and concern and trust between ourselves and our children, and creating social arrangements in which children will be valued and well cared for, are more important than maximizing individual utilities. And the moral theories that might be compatible with such assumptions might be very different from those with which we are familiar.

▶ NOTES

1. Virginia Held, *Rights and Goods: Justifying Social Action* (New York: Free Press, 1984). [V.H.]
2. *polis:* state, political society [D.C.A., ed.]
3. Nancy Hartsock, *Money, Sex, and Power* (New York: Longman, 1983), p. 39. [V.H.]
4. Lawrence A. Blum, *Friendship, Altruism and Morality* (London: Routledge & Kegan Paul, 1980), p. 1. [V.H.]
5. Nell Noddings, *Caring: A Feminist Approach to Ethics and Moral Education* (Berkeley: University of California Press, 1984), pp. 91–94. [V.H.]
6. According to the *categorical imperative,* the personal policy on which our action is based should be one that we can consistently will that all persons follow; according to the *principle of utility,* we should act in a way that maximizes utility (the greatest happiness of the greatest number). [D.C.A.]
7. *utility:* the experience of happiness or pleasure [D.C.A.]

Just Caring

Rita Manning

Rita Manning is Professor of Philosophy at San José State University in San José, California. She earned her doctorate in philosophy at the University of California, Riverside, in 1982, writing a dissertation entitled *The Moral Responsibility of Collectives.* She is the author of *Speaking from the Heart: A Feminist Perspective on Ethics* (1992) and coeditor (with René Trujillo) of *Social Justice in a Diverse Society* (1996).

Our reading is Manning's 1992 article, "Just Caring," which proposes and defends an "ethic of caring." (For an expanded version of this article, see Chapter 4 of *Speaking from the Heart.*) The ethic of caring, Manning explains, has two components: a disposition to care and an obligation to express this disposition through actions (to "care for"). When I encounter a person, animal, value, institution, or object that cannot meet a need without help, I should have a disposition to care. How I translate this disposition into actions "depends on my ability to care for, my obligation to care for myself, and my sense of the appropriateness of the need and the best way to meet it." Manning points out that I am not obliged to spend all my energy caring for others; the ethic of care includes an obligation to care for myself as well.

What role do rules and rights play in the ethic of care? Rules provide a minimum standard for morality, and rights give a certain protection to the helpless. Rules and rights can aid us as we deliberate how to care for other beings. When a person in need does not want us to respond according to a generally accepted rule, we should listen carefully to the person and be willing to ignore the rule, if that is what caring requires in this situation.

Manning explains that because we live in a largely uncaring society, caring persons face the danger of "caring burnout." To avoid experiencing burnout, individuals must remember to take time to care for themselves as well as others. A long-term way to reduce the risk of burnout by caring persons is to reduce the number of unmet needs in society by working to make cultural and social institutions more caring-based.

▼

In this essay, I shall sketch and provide a cursory defense of a model of ethical considerations which I shall call, following Nel Noddings, an ethic of caring.[1]

I shall confess at the outset that this model owes more to my experience as a woman, a teacher, and a mother than to my training and experience in moral philosophy. Over the years, my students have convinced me of the barrenness of standard ethical theories. It has occurred to me only very recently that, in sketching a more adequate model, I might appeal to my own experience as a moral person. I credit Hume,[2] Annette Baier,[3] and Carol Gilligan[4] with waking me from my dogmatic slumber and Nel Noddings with allowing me to take caring, which is central to my moral experience, seriously.

An ethic of caring, as I shall defend it, includes two elements. First is a disposition to care. This is a willingness to receive others, a willingness to give the lucid attention to the needs of others which filling these needs appropriately requires. I see this disposition to care as nourished by a spiritual awareness similar to the awareness argued for by proponents of the women's spirituality movement. As Starhawk describes this awareness: "Immanent justice rests on the first principle of magic: all things are interconnected. All is relationship. Perhaps the ultimate ethic of immanence is to choose to make that relationship one of love, . . . love for all the eternally self-creating world, love of the light and the mysterious darkness, and raging love against all that would diminish the unspeakable beauty of the world."[5]

In addition to being sensitive to my place in the world and to my general obligation to be a caring person, I am also obligated to care for. (I am following Noddings in using "care for" to indicate caring as expressed in action.) In the paradigm case, caring for involves acting in some appropriate way to respond to the needs of persons, and animals, but can also be extended to responding to the needs of communities, values, or objects. My obligation to care for is limited by a principle of supererogation,[6] which is necessary to keep an ethic of caring from degenerating into an ethics of total self-sacrifice. I shall argue that we are obligated to adopt this model of caring as far as we can in our moral deliberations. We are morally permitted and sometimes morally obliged to appeal to rules and rights. In Gilligan's idiom, we are required to listen to the voices of both care and justice. In what follows, I shall first fill in some of the details of this model. Specifically, I shall discuss what it is to care for someone or something and when we are obligated to care for. Next, I shall say something about the role of rules and rights in this model.

I. Caring

I have often wondered if taking a class in moral philosophy was the best way for students to become sensitive to moral concerns. It seemed to me that a better way would be to have students work in soup kitchens or shelters for the homeless. I am convinced that taking care of my children has made me more open to moral concerns. In taking care of the hungry, homeless, and helpless, we are engaged in caring for. In the standard case, caring for is immediate; it admits of no surrogates. When I directly care for some creature, I am in physical contact. Our eyes meet, our hands touch. Not every need can be met in this immediate way. In that case, I must accept a surrogate. Not every need can be met by individual action. In those cases, I must seek collective action. But when I can do the caring for myself, I ought to do so, at least some of the time. The need of the other may sometimes require that I do the caring for. If my child needs my attention, I cannot meet this need by sending her to a therapist. Even when the needs of the other do not require my personal attention, I must provide some of the caring for directly in order to develop and sustain my ability to care.

My day-to-day interactions with other persons create a web of reciprocal caring. In these interactions, I am obliged to be a caring person. I am free, to a certain extent, to choose when and how to care for these others. My choice is limited by my relationships with these others and by their needs. A pressing need calls up an immediate obligation to care for; roles and responsibilities call up an obligation to respond in a caring manner. In the first case, I am obligated (though this obligation can be limited by a principle of supererogation) to respond; in the second, I can choose, within limits, when and how to care.

A creature in need who is unable to meet this need without help calls for a caring response on my part. This response needn't always be direct. Sometimes it is better to organize a political response. (Many, for example, who are confronted on the street by homeless people are unsure about how to respond, convinced that their immediate response will not be enough, might even be counterproductive.) Certain relationships obligate me to provide direct caring for. When my daughter falls and asks me to "kiss it and make it better," I can't send her to my neighbor for the kiss.

My roles as mother, as teacher, as volunteer, put me in particular relationships to others. These roles require and sustain caring. My obligation to my infant children and my animals is to meet their basic needs for physical sustenance (food, shelter, clothing, health care) and for companionship and love. My obligation to my students is grounded on my roles as teacher and philosopher and their psychological needs to discover who they are and how they can live with integrity. Here I feel a connection with my students but also with teaching and philosophy. But if one of my students comes to me needing another kind of care, I may be obligated to provide it, though I may not be obligated to do so singlehandedly. My response depends on my ability to care for, my obligation to care for myself, and my sense of the appropriateness of the need and the best way to meet it.

In discharging obligations to care for that are based on role responsibility, I am conscious of my need to fill those roles conscientiously. The role of teacher, for example, requires a certain impartiality; the role of mother requires a fierce devotion to each particular child. But I am free, to a certain extent, to choose my roles. In adopting or reshaping roles, I should be sensitive to my need to be cared for as well as my capacity to care. In critiquing socially designed and assigned roles, we should aim for roles and divisions of roles that make caring more likely to occur.

Caring for can involve a measure of self-sacrifice. The rescuers of Jessica McClure[7] who went without sleep for days, the parents of an infant who go without uninterrupted sleep for months, are involved in caring for. Caring for involves an openness to the one cared for. Caring for requires that I see the real need and that I satisfy it insofar as I am able. In satisfying it, I am sensitive not just to the need but to the feelings of those in need.

Caring for does not require that I feel any particular emotion toward the one cared for, but that I am open to the possibility that some emotional attachment may form in the caring for. Nor does it require that I have an ongoing relationship with the one cared for. I may meet the one cared for as stranger, though the caring for will change that.

Obviously, a model of caring along the lines I am defending must include an account of needs. I cannot offer a complete account here, but I would draw heavily from biology, psychology, and other relevant social sciences in constructing such an account; there would be an essentially normative component as well. I want to begin by drawing a distinction between what I will call subsistence needs and psychological needs. Subsistence needs will usually be needs that must be filled if physical existence is to continue. Psychological needs are needs that must be filled if human flourishing is to occur. Filling subsistence needs does not automatically benefit both the carer and the cared for. Rather, the carer is likely to feel burdened by filling such needs, though the recognition that one has filled such needs often creates a sense of virtue in the carer. I am reminded here of the ferocious demands for food that infants make on their parents with astonishing regularity. Filling psychological needs can often be more fulfilling. It is more likely to be done in a reciprocal relationship and in such a relationship filling psychological needs requires that both parties share the roles of carer and cared for. I needn't respond to every need. In choosing how and when to respond, I should consider the seriousness of the need, the benefit to the one needing care of filling this particular need, and the competing needs of others, including myself, that will be affected by my filling this particular need.

II. Objects of Care

I can care for persons, animals, values, institutions, and objects. My choice of objects of caring about should reflect my own need to be cared for and my capacity to care. But decisions about what to care for should not depend exclusively on my own needs and capacities. I should also be sensitive to the needs that summon the obligation to care for. If I understand my obligation to care for as following from the existence of need and helplessness, I should care for institutions, values, and practices that would diminish such needs. One might argue that we could virtually eliminate the need to care for by creating such institutions, values, and practices and hence undermine our capacity to care. But even in a perfectly just world, children would need care and people and animals would get sick. Furthermore, human needs include more than needs for physical sustenance. Human needs for companionship and intimacy would exist even in a world free from the horrors of war, homelessness, sickness, and disease.

III. Defense of a General Obligation to Care

The obligation to respond as carer when appropriate can be defended on three grounds. The first is the need. Here I would appeal to Peter Singer's principle, "if it is in our power to prevent something very bad happening without thereby sacrificing anything of comparable moral significance, we ought to do it."[8]

The second is the recognition that human relationships require a continuous kind of caring. This caring involves three components: being receptive to the other, being accepting of the other, and being on-call for the other when s/he is in need.[9] Unless we want to do away with human relationships, we must be open to the demands of caring that such relationships require. But caring in human relationships is, as human relationships are, reciprocal.

The third defense is that I cannot develop and sustain my ability to care unless I do some active caring. This is an empirical claim and we must look both to social science and to our own experience in evaluating it, but there is an obvious way in which caring for enhances our ability to care. When I make the real attempt to care for, I must understand the needs of the one cared for. I must also see how that one wants the needs to be addressed. This ability to notice needs and wants, to empathize as well as sympathize, is developed through caring. Of course, one might ask why one should want to develop this capacity to care. It seems to me that the right response is to point out that human lives devoid of caring impulses and responses would be nasty, brutish, short, and lonely.[10]

IV. Limitations on Obligations to Care

I don't think that we are obligated to be like Mother Teresa.[11] Mother Teresa cares for continuously. We can limit our obligation to care for by focusing on the defenses of this obligation. First, I have a prima facie obligation[12] to care for when I come across a creature in need who is unable to meet that need without help, when my caring is called on as a part of a reciprocal relationship, or when indicated as part of my role responsibility. My actual obligation rests on the seriousness of the need, my assessment of the appropriateness of filling the need, and my ability to do something about filling it. But I must also recognize that I am a person who must be cared for and that I must recognize and respond to my own need to be cared for. The continuous caring for required to respond to needs for physical sustenance is, for most of us, incompatible with caring for ourselves. But not all caring for involves responding to physical needs. The caring for required to sustain relationships, which is usually reciprocal, can be a source of great strength to the person doing the caring for. Finally, allowing myself to suffer caring burnout also diminishes my ability to care for others in the future. I don't mean to argue that caring for requires no sacrifice. Indeed, where the need is great and my ability to meet it sufficient, I am required to sacrifice. But I am not required to adopt this as a form of life.

My obligation to care for is not an all-or-nothing thing. Being unable to care for now does not eliminate the possibility that I may be obligated to meet this need later. This is a general point about obligations. I might owe someone money and be unable to pay it back now, through no fault of my own. If I later come into a windfall, I am obligated to pay the money back then. In addition, there is no one right way to care for. My assessment of the appropriateness of the need, my ability to meet the need, and my sense of the most successful way of doing so provide some guidance here. Perhaps immediate caring for is the best way to meet a need in one case, and cooperative political activity the most successful way of meeting other needs. I would want to leave these kinds of choices up to the agent.

V. Rules and Rights

In my model, rules and rights serve three purposes. They can be used to persuade, to sketch a moral minimum below which no one should fall and beyond which behavior is condemned, and they can be used to deliberate in some cases.

My attention to rules and rights here does not reflect an unwillingness to make appeals to virtues and practices. I think it is fair to describe caring as a virtue. I do include other virtues and practices as fulfilling each of the three functions that rules and rights play in my model. We certainly can and do persuade by reminding others of virtues: "Would an honest man do that?" We likewise persuade by pointing to practices: "Native Americans don't have that kind of an attitude about the earth." Virtues and practices can serve as minimums: "I can see that you won't be doing me any favors, but at least give me the courtesy of an honest reply."

We don't live in a caring world. By that I mean that not everyone recognizes his or her obligation to care. Our society does not encourage the flourishing of this capacity, but undermines it in various ways. In a world infamous for its lack of caring, we need tools of persuasion to protect the helpless. This is one of the roles that rules and rights fill. We can reason in the language of rules with those who lack a sufficient degree of caring. If their natural sympathies are not engaged by the presence of suffering, we can attempt to appeal to reason: "How would you feel if you were in their place?" "What would be the consequences of such behavior on a large scale?" I am not convinced of the effect of such persuasion, and it is, I think, an empirical question whether such appeals would persuade where caring did not, but I suspect that such socially agreed-on minimums could serve as persuasive appeals.

Rules and rights provide a minimum below which no one should fall and beyond which behavior is morally condemned. Rules provide a minimum standard for morality. Rights provide a measure of protection for the helpless. But on this level of moral discourse, morality is, like politics, the art of the possible. In the face of large-scale selfishness and inattention, perhaps the best we can hope for is a minimum below which no one should fall and beyond which behavior is roundly condemned. But we shouldn't fool ourselves into thinking that staying above this minimum is a sufficient condition for being a morally decent person. I don't want to deny the importance of these socially agreed-on minimums; in a less than perfect world, they provide some real protection. They are not, in principle, incompatible with caring but can, I think, encourage caring. Much caring requires collective action and without a shared sense of moral minimums it will be difficult to organize such collective action.

Elizabeth Wolgast, in *The Grammar of Justice,* argues against the claim that treating patients in a moral fashion is entirely a matter of respecting their rights.[13] She points out that patients are often sick and in need of caring for. In this situation, she argues, we want doctors and other health-care workers to care for the patient. This involves far more than respecting rights. One could talk, I suppose, about a patient's right to be cared for, but as Wolgast points out, rights talk suggests a minimum below which the doctor should not fall, and in this case, we are less interested in the minimum than in the maximum. We want all our moral citizens to be open to the obligation to care for.

Rules and rights can also be used to deliberate under some conditions. Often we don't need to appeal to rules in deciding whom to care for and how to care for them. A creature's need and our ability to meet it identifies it as a candidate for caring for. We decide how to care for by appeal to the need, the strategies for meeting it, and the desires of the one in need about how best to meet the need. But when I am not in direct contact with the objects of care, my actions cannot be guided by the expressed and observed desires of those cared for, and hence I might want to appeal to rules. In these cases, I must make assumptions about their desires. I shall assume that they do not wish to fall below some minimum. Rules that provide a minimum standard for acceptable behavior ought to be sensitive to the general desires and aims of creatures, so I may take these into account. I am also free to appeal to my needs for care and on that basis decide that I do not wish to violate some socially approved minimum standard of behavior. I can also appeal to rules and rights when care must be allocated. For example, in a hospital emergency room we must make sure that the needs of the first accident victim of the night do not cause us to ignore the later victims. Finally, since rules and rights can express a consensus about morally acceptable behavior, I should be sensitive to the expectations generated in the one cared for by the public recognition of such roles and rights. For example, suppose I want to make sure that my family and friends are happy and involved in the wedding of my son. I might be tempted to ignore the rules of etiquette in making sure that my guests are uniquely provided for. But if the mother of the bride feels slighted because I didn't treat her the way she expected to be treated (that is, as the etiquette rules say you should treat the mother of the bride), then I haven't really responded to her in a caring manner.

One might argue here that meeting some expressed needs might violate the moral minimums in our society. I am willing to grant that this can happen. If it does, we must remember that the rules do not have a life of their own, but are guides. They help us to formulate a caring response because they speak to us of what most of us would want as a caring response in a similar situation. If the one needing care does not want the response suggested by the appropriate rule, we should listen to him or her very carefully and be willing to ignore the rule. For example, suppose someone wanted us to help him/her commit suicide. I suspect that ideally we could and should settle this kind of a case without appealing to rules. Instead, we should appeal to the facts of the case. Is the person terminally ill or merely depressed? These conditions require different remedies. In the first case, one might be doing the right thing to aid in the suicide. Here, one must count the cost to oneself, as well as the needs and desires of the one cared for. In the second case, we appeal beyond the expressed needs to the unexpressed needs. This person probably needs some other care. Here, we make every attempt to listen to this person, to understand his or her pain, but we also remind ourselves that suicide is the final option for dealing with pain. We make this decision, not by appeal to a rule, but by reminding ourselves of the times when we or someone we know came close to suicide. We remember how it felt and how it was resolved.

In some cases, though, I cannot respond as one caring. As I approach caring burnout, I can then appeal to rules and rights. I do not want my behavior to fall below some minimum standard, nor do I want the one in need of care to fall below some moral minimum.

In the ideal caring society with sufficient resources to meet needs and to provide for some sort of flourishing, each of us would spend roughly the same amount of time being cared for. We would experience this as children and as adults. Hence, we would be surrounded by a nexus of caring. We would be persons who cared for and were supported by a history of being cared for. We would be free, to some extent, to choose whom to care for because there would be others to provide for needs and for flourishing. We would not be totally free, because social roles would commit us to some responsibilities to care. It's not clear that rules and rights would play a very big part in this world, but this is certainly not the world in which we live.

The people in our world differ in their ability and their willingness to care for others. Since I am both a creature who can care and a creature who needs care, I would, if I were committed to caring, be faced with enormous needs for care while sometimes suffering from a lack of caring for myself. This is true even if we grant that the kind of caring (in particular, psychological caring) involved in reciprocal relationships sustains all parties in the relationship. But since such relationships don't come easily and naturally, I would have to spend some time and energy establishing a nexus of care to support myself. In creating and maintaining this nexus of care, I would be developing bonds and responsibilities of care.

But spending much of one's time getting one's own needs for care satisfied leaves little time for caring for others. At the same time, everyone else is in much the same boat. And the gross inequality in the distribution of resources means that many slip between the caring cracks and into dire need. This puts the caring person in a bind. Real need presents itself to a person who is often running a caring deficit of his or her own. Caring burnout results. The only way to effectively reduce caring burnout is to change cultural and social institutions toward a model of caring. This is not the path that our culture has taken. Instead we careen from me-first-isms to paroxysms of guilt about the tremendous needs that have resulted. We make renewed commitments to care which are rejected as softheaded a generation later.

What are caring persons to do? Caring persons should try to respond to need by caring for, but they must pay attention to their own needs for care. They must navigate through an uncaring world without falling into total caring burnout. They should work for institutions, cultures, and practices that would reduce subsistence needs by redistributing resources and increasing the supply of caretakers, and they should encourage social change toward a culture of reciprocity in meeting psychological needs. But while struggling in our pre-caring world, caring persons are not obligated to care until they slip into caring burnout. This denies their own status as persons who deserve care and is counterproductive. It diminishes, in the long run, the amount of care they can provide. As they approach caring burnout, they should refill their care tanks by taking care of their own needs. During this period of renewal, they are still required to respect the moral minimums represented by rules and rights.

I haven't talked about what the rules and rights should be. In drafting a set of rules and rights, I should be sensitive to two considerations. The first is that rules and rights provide a moral minimum. The second is that rules and rights reflect a consensus about moral minimums. In this sense, morality is the art of the possible.

The morally preferred way to live is to appeal to caring. This suggests that rules and rights should reflect a sense of what counts as need, and a conception of flourishing, and a recognition of what would usually be accepted, by the ones cared for, as appropriate ways of responding to need and providing for flourishing. Notions of need and flourishing ought to be sensitive to empirical considerations about human nature, interaction, social organization, and so on, but they also have an irreducibly normative component. A defense of rules and rights would need to defend this normative component. We would also want rules and rights that would provide a climate for moral growth toward a caring society.

Rules and rights do play an important role in my ethics of caring, but we shouldn't forget that our primary responsibility is to care for. If this means that we are often unsure about just what to do, then we must live with this uncertainty. Discovering what to do requires that we listen carefully to the ones cared for. We should also recognize that it is often painful to be confronted by those in need, and even by those whom we could enrich. Appealing to rules provides a measure of security for ourselves, but we shouldn't allow it to distance us from the objects of care.

▶ NOTES

1. I owe a special debt to Nel Noddings, whose powerful defense of caring inspired me to take caring seriously: *Caring: A Feminine Approach to Ethics and Moral Education* (Berkeley: University of California Press, 1984). [R.M.]

2. Hume argued that the task of moral philosophy ought to be to look reflexively at actual moral practice. [R.M.] David Hume (1711–1776) was a Scottish philosopher and historian. [D.C.A., ed.]

3. Annette Baier argues forcefully that we should pay exclusive attention to reforming current moral practices. See *Postures of the Mind: Essays on Mind and Morals* (Minneapolis: University of Minnesota Press, 1985), especially Chapters 11–15. [R.M.]

4. Carol Gilligan, *In a Different Voice: Psychological Theory and Women's Development* (Cambridge, Mass.: Harvard University Press, 1982). [R.M.]

5. Starhawk, *Dreaming the Dark: Magic, Sex and Politics* (Boston: Beacon Press, 1982), p. 44. [R.M.]

6. *supererogation:* doing more than is required by duty or obligation. [D.C.A.]

7. In 1987 the baby Jessica McClure was rescued after being trapped for nearly 60 hours in a 22-foot hole into which she had fallen in Midland, Texas. [D.C.A.]

8. Peter Singer, *Practical Ethics* (Cambridge, England: Cambridge University Press, 1979), p. 168. [R.M.]

9. This analysis is from Milton Mayeroff, *On Caring* (New York: Harper & Row, 1971). [R.M.]

10. Manning refers here to the famous remark by the English philosopher Thomas Hobbes (1588–1679) that before the formation of society and government, human life was "solitary, poor, nasty, brutish, and short" (Thomas Hobbes, *Leviathan,* Part I, Chapter XIII). [D.C.A.]

11. Mother Teresa (1910–1997) was an Albanian-born Roman Catholic nun who devoted her life to caring for the poor and dying in India. [D.C.A.]

12. *prima facie obligation:* an obligation that holds unless it is overridden by another, stronger obligation. [D.C.A.]

13. Elizabeth H. Wolgast, *The Grammar of Justice* (Ithaca, N.Y.: Cornell University Press, 1987), Chapter 3. [R.M.]

Credits